Water Allocation]

This book analyses water allocation law and policy in New Zealand and offers a comparative analysis with Australia. In New Zealand, it is generally accepted that water allocation law has failed to be adequately addressed and New Zealand is now faced with the problem of over-allocation in many catchments. In comparison, Australia has extensive experience in reforming its water law and policy over the last 20 years. This book provides a comparative and critical analysis of the lessons that New Zealand can learn from the Australian experience and offers guidance for the improvement of water allocation outcomes in New Zealand. Starting with the background of water allocation law and policy in New Zealand, the book traces the evolution of legal policies, including the 1967 Water and Soil Conservation Act and the 1991 Resource Management Act, and examines the role they have played in current water allocation issues. The book situates these findings within global challenges, such as the impact of climate change, and the global scarcity of and increasing demand for freshwater resources.

This book will be of great interest to students and scholars researching water law and policy, natural resource management and environmental law more broadly. It will also be of use to policy makers and professionals involved in developing and implementing water allocation laws and policies.

Jagdeepkaur Singh-Ladhar is a Lecturer at the University of Auckland, New Zealand.

Earthscan Studies in Water Resource Management

The Biopolitics of Water
Governance, Scarcity and Populations
Sofie Hellberg

Water, Technology and the Nation-State
Edited by Filippo Menga and Erik Swyngedouw

Revitalizing Urban Waterway Communities
Streams of Environmental Justice
Richard Smardon, Sharon Moran and April Baptiste

Water, Creativity and Meaning
Multidisciplinary Understandings of Human-Water Relationships
Edited by Liz Roberts and Katherine Phillips

Water, Climate Change and the Boomerang Effect
Unintentional Consequences for Resource Insecurity
Edited by Larry Swatuk and Lars Wirkus

Legal Rights for Rivers
Competition, Collaboration and Water Governance
Erin O'Donnell

Water Allocation Law in New Zealand
Lessons from Australia
Jagdeepkaur Singh-Ladhar

For more information about this series, please visit: http://www.routledge. com/books/series/ECWRM/

Water Allocation Law in New Zealand
Lessons from Australia

Jagdeepkaur Singh-Ladhar

Routledge
Taylor & Francis Group
LONDON AND NEW YORK

from Routledge

First published 2020
by Routledge
2 Park Square, Milton Park, Abingdon, Oxon OX14 4RN

and by Routledge
52 Vanderbilt Avenue, New York, NY 10017

Routledge is an imprint of the Taylor & Francis Group, an informa business

© 2020 Jagdeepkaur Singh-Ladhar

The right of Jagdeepkaur Singh-Ladhar to be identified as author of this
work has been asserted by them in accordance with sections 77 and 78 of the
Copyright, Designs and Patents Act 1988.

British Library Cataloguing-in-Publication Data
A catalogue record for this book is available from the British Library

Library of Congress Cataloging-in-Publication Data
Names: Singh-Ladhar, Jagdeepkaur, author.
Title: Water allocation law in New Zealand: lessons from Australia /
Jagdeepkaur Singh-Ladhar.
Description: Abingdon, Oxon; New York, NY: Routledge, 2020. |
Series: Earthscan studies in water resource management | Based on author's
thesis (doctoral-University of Waikato, 2019) issued under title: Improving
water allocation law and policy in New Zealand: lessons from Australia. |
Includes bibliographical references and index. |
Identifiers: LCCN 2020008044 (print) | LCCN 2020008045 (ebook) |
ISBN 9780367896621 (hardback) | ISBN 9781003020394 (ebook)
Subjects: LCSH: Water resources development–Law and legislation–
New Zealand. | Water-supply–Law and legislation–New Zealand. |
Water resources development–Law and legislation–Australia. |
Water-supply–Law and legislation–Australia. | Law–New Zealand–Australian
influences.
Classification: LCC KUQ2522 .S56 2020 (print) | LCC KUQ2522 (ebook) |
DDC 346.9304/691–dc23
LC record available at https://lccn.loc.gov/2020008044
LC ebook record available at https://lccn.loc.gov/2020008045

ISBN: 978-0-367-89662-1 (hbk)
ISBN: 978-0-367-51867-7 (pbk)
ISBN: 978-1-003-02039-4 (ebk)

Typeset in Times New Roman
by Deanta Global Publishing Services, Chennai, India

Contents

1 Introduction   1

2 The water allocation policy gap 1991–2011   14

3 New Zealand water allocation law and policy after 2011   51

4 Australian water allocation law and policy   66

5 Comparative analysis   111

6 Conclusion   138

   Index   145

1 Introduction

Understanding the global context of water allocation

The problem of increasing global water scarcity

Water scarcity is a critical issue. A recent high profile example in early 2018 was the water scarcity issues experienced by Cape Town when it was predicted that the city would run out of water.[1] While the issues in Cape Town were intertwined with other infrastructure, social, political and environmental issues, there is sufficient research to show that water scarcity is an impending problem for other cities too.[2] As a starting point, it is important to understand that freshwater is a limited resource. Statistics show that of the total available amount of freshwater on Earth, approximately only 1% of it is suitable for human use.[3] Then of the 1% that is suitable for human use, there are further issues relating to water access and water quality. In addition, the distribution of water and rainfall patterns also contributes to water availability and scarcity. Projections of water scarcity referred to below confirm that the extent of water scarcity may vary but that this "wicked" problem will not resolve itself without policy interventions.[4]

As the discussion below will show, it is generally accepted that not all the water physically available should be allocated. The definition of water scarcity is complex and includes taking into consideration when water is available, the location of water, the ease of obtaining access to water and the water quality.[5] Water scarcity can be measured on a scale of water availability per capita. The Falkenmark Water Stress Indicator provides a threshold of 1,700 cubic metres of renewable water annually for each person in a country as a minimum requirement.[6] According to the indicator, countries below this threshold are experiencing "water stress", countries with a level below 1,000 cubic metres have "water scarcity" and finally countries below 500 cubic metres have "absolute scarcity". The different measures are an indicator of physical water scarcity.

Water scarcity defined from a hydrological perspective makes a clear connection with the water cycle. Hydrological studies assert that both surface water and groundwater supplies are placed under increased pressure as demand increases. They confirm that groundwater supplies are particularly vulnerable as groundwater storage "provides a natural buffer against water shortage".[7] However, groundwater depletion is more difficult to observe in comparison to surface water depletion and demand for groundwater increases when surface water supplies are inadequate.[8] These themes are also present in the example of Australian water law reform in the Murray-Darling Basin.

The more commonly used definitions of water scarcity in water allocation policy focus on economic water scarcity rather than on the physical water scarcity discussed above. Even within the literature on economic water scarcity, there is "no commonly accepted definition of water scarcity"; however, there are factors that can be taken into consideration to measure water scarcity.[9] These include the human and environmental demand for water and whether there is adequate water available to meet those needs. Water availability also depends on the variable weather patterns. Economic concepts of water scarcity attempt to measure and model the demand and availability of water before it becomes physically scarce. Ultimately, all measures of water scarcity form the context of water allocation law and policy which aims to allocate a predetermined limit of water across users.

The definition and measurement of water scarcity are relevant to understanding the water law and policy of Australia and New Zealand as there are relative differences in the type of water scarcity experienced by each country. On the one hand, the Australian experience relates generally to physical water scarcity for the environment alongside economic water scarcity for irrigators and other users,[10] whilst, on the other hand, urban demand for water would be an example of water scarcity in relation to basic human needs. In contrast, New Zealand is experiencing problems with over-allocation and limited means to reallocate water to higher- value uses.[11]

Global responses to the water scarcity problem

A key problem is the ability to deal with increasing global scarcity of water as human demand increases. The challenges are identified as developing good freshwater management practice, changes in hydrology and the growing demand for freshwater.[12] One solution put forward by the United Nations is to focus on water in the Sustainable Development Goals. In 2014, the United Nations released its revised goals for global development which include the sustainable use of water.[13] The "water-energy-food nexus has become central to the discussions" on developing and implementing these goals.[14] The United

Nations Water branch provides support to countries implementing water reform and will monitor the goals.[15] In September 2016, the United Nations released an "Action Plan" for water based on Sustainable Development Goal 6 for the "availability and sustainable management of water and sanitation for all".[16] Goal 6.4 measures the available quantity of water but it also needs to make a stronger link with water quality.[17] The High Level Panel responsible for delivering Sustainable Development Goal 6 includes political representatives, including the Prime Minister of Australia.[18] The inclusion of political representatives therefore shows that water allocation is also a political problem.

The High Level Plan on Water defined water needs broadly; these range from water for sanitation and safe drinking to planning for water for the future. The plan identified risks from adverse events such as droughts and floods that are more likely to occur in the future. In addition, demographic changes and decisions about how water is allocated will contribute negatively to the problem of water scarcity on a global scale:[19]

> Changes in human populations and settlements, as well as increasing demand for agriculture purposes will exacerbate scarcity problems, as will poor decisions on water allocation and use. 45% of total GDP is projected to be at risk due to water stress by 2050.

This statistic on water allocation illustrates the extent to which freshwater allocation is a fundamental global issue. The United Nations is focused on finding solutions that rely upon good decision making to address water scarcity problems by taking into account the interrelationships in the water-energy-food nexus.

Despite international commitments to addressing water scarcity, problems with developing a targeted water policy remain:[20]

> The political commitments acknowledge[d] the important role water plays in sustainable development. However, the discourse of water and sustainable development homogenises the problem of water scarcity, when in fact the causes of scarcity are not uniform and not simply a matter to be solved through mechanisms to deal with economic goods.

The water-energy-food nexus requires an analysis of factors such as the input of energy into water systems. A water system can be "energy intensive" in itself if water needs to be moved across long distances[21] and includes, for example, the use of desalination plants, which are recognised as an "energy intensive approach to freshwater production".[22]

On the other hand, it is also important to recognise water inputs into energy systems. Any decision to establish an energy plant should take into account the "total amount of water, calculated on a whole-system basis"[23] which, in practice, means that a commitment to increase biofuels should include the total amount of water used to grow the biofuel crop, if that is the source of the fuel.[24] Many of these calculations are based on economic theory or models. The use of economics as a means to address water allocation issues is examined in more detail in the Australian chapter.

New Zealand and Australia's response to managing water

New Zealand and Australia have both made efforts to introduce principles of sustainability to their environmental law.[25] Australian studies have identified continued improvement in sustainability outcomes in a multi-level governance framework which relies heavily on effective state cooperation.[26] An empirical study of principles of ecological sustainability in water plans shows that sustainability was an important factor in developing plans for the Murray-Darling River Basin in Australia.[27] New Zealand's commitment to sustainability in the purpose section of the RMA is well documented.[28] On the other hand, there are also accounts of the challenges to implementing sustainable water allocation, particularly from a governance perspective.[29] As in Australia, the implementation of water law reform from the national to regional level are issues at the forefront of challenges to sustainable water allocation in New Zealand.

The primary legislation regulating water allocation in New Zealand is the Resource Management Act 1991 (RMA). At the time it was implemented, the Act led the world in implementing principles of sustainability in environmental planning and natural resource allocation.[30] Extensive environmental law reform preceded its enactment with expectations that it would improve resource allocation, including water allocation.[31] However, the reality has been quite different. It is now clear that the current problems with water allocation under the RMA were unforeseen and over-allocation is one of the problems to emerge from this context.[32]

The problems facing New Zealand water allocation law and policy are due to several contributing factors. The most predominant of these factors is the failure to fully implement the RMA. For 20 years, from 1991 until 2011, New Zealand did not have national guidance on water policy.[33] During this time, a "gap" in water allocation law and policy existed. Under the Resource Management Act 1991 (RMA), central and local government had the statutory function of establishing rules for resource management according to policies and principles within a hierarchical structure.[34] These plans and policies ideally should have included rules and policies for water allocation. At the top of the structure for water allocation, there should have been a relevant National Policy Statement to ensure that the RMA was fully implemented.[35] After several failed attempts, the government developed the first National Policy Statement for Freshwater Management in 2011. It was amended in 2014 and revised in 2017.

The water policy gap from 1991 until 2011 contributed to the emergence of a default model of water allocation. Water permit applications were prioritised by time following the "first in, first served" precedent established in *Fleetwing Farms v Marlborough District Council*.[36] Water allocation by priority of time and the policy gap have contributed to contemporary water allocation problems facing New Zealand.

In those catchments that are fully allocated or over-allocated and the "first in, first served" method of water allocation which leaves limited scope to reallocate water to higher-value uses.[37] This book examines how to address New Zealand's water allocation problems which emerged during the water policy gap from 1991 to 2011.

Key definitions

One point of language use worth addressing is to simplify the understanding of "water allocation" as a term used in this book. Readers will be assisted by looking at the definition of the word "allocation". An "allocation" may be either the "act of setting aside" something or "that which is allocated to a particular person".[38] In New Zealand as understood in a general sense – pursuant to the RMA the term "water allocation" is the grant of a consent in the form of a water permit by the Crown to take and use water at a particular location to the applicant, such as an individual or company. The volume of water allocated under a water permit is the "water allocation", which is usually a fixed amount, unless the regional council has made rules that affect the reliability of that water permit. In Australia, the term "water allocation" is used in a general sense to refer to the system of distribution of water. Under the National Water Initiative (NWI) reforms, however, the equivalent term is a "water entitlement", which refers to a legal right to access water in the form of a "water licence". The amount received under the water licence is not the same as the volume of water actually received. This distinction is due to the introduction of concepts that relate to sharing water. Typically, the holder of a water entitlement will not receive a set volume of water, instead they will receive a pro-rate seasonal or annual share of the water available to be allocated. This process of determining the volume of water delivered or pumped under the water entitlement is what is commonly referred to as "water allocation" in the Australian literature.

A word is needed to avoid confusion about the term "unbundling". Unbundling is a term that is used in different ways. The meaning ascribed to it evolves. At times it is used to mean the separation of a water allocation

from land. This use is often found in non-legal literature on water allocation. At other times it is used in its correct legal sense, which is the separation of the right to take water from the right to use it. To avoid confusion
in this research, both definitions are used according to the context of the
writing. The former is used more so where there is a policy discussion. The
latter is used more in the Australian section of the book where water rights
have actually been unbundled in the correct legal sense.

There is a compound understanding of unbundling which is best illustrated by Australian experience in water allocation law reform. In a fully
unbundled system, the water take and use can be further unbundled so that
new types of water products are created. The more recent water allocation
reforms in Australia provide an example of how full unbundling can occur.
For example, a fully unbundled system can set the volume of water allocation that will be physically delivered to each water licence holder at the
catchment level. A fully unbundled system will have a seasonal water allocation determined for a catchment, usually as a percentage of the water that
licence holders are entitled to receive under their water licence.

Research limitations

A limitation of this research is that it does not address the role of Māori claims
relating to water. Wheen observed the marginalised role of Māori in the history of water law.[39] Wheen states that any pre-existing notions of Māori
customary law were not acknowledged when common law was applied by
the Courts.[40] This stance was continued as it was "ignored or avoided as
introduced common law was applied".[41] Preliminary research includes an
extensive literature review undertaken on the interpretation of water-related
law and Māori customary law.[42] In the Australian context, greater inclusion
of indigenous participation in water allocation is one of the challenges of the
more recent reforms.[43] Māori customary law has not been used for the allocation of water by the New Zealand government. Its treatment is beyond the
scope of this book. However, the role of Māori in water law in New Zealand
is worthy of separate attention as an area of future research.

While this book does not address issues relating to Māori claims, it is
conceded that this issue has come into much sharper focus over the time
that this research was undertaken. Even if this dimension was acknowledged as part of the scope of the research, the question of water allocation
remains to be addressed. The present method of water allocation is unsustainable regardless of who holds the allocation. Indeed, the lack of politics
to address water allocation may be in part due to the associated questions
about the role of Māori in water allocation and the complexity of finding
answers.

The Crown is in ongoing discussions with the Iwi Leaders Group and Iwi Chairs regarding freshwater-related discussions. The Cabinet position was initially that no one can own freshwater, including the Crown, which preserves the common law position on water ownership. It has also stated that there will not be a national settlement of freshwater claims on a national level and that generally looking forward to the next stage of freshwater reforms there will be a provision for including iwi/hapu rights and interests.[44] In 2018, these "bottom lines" were updated to include the common interest of improving water quality and quantity, and while no one owns freshwater, there is a guardianship role for all to look after freshwater resources.[45] There was specific reference to the high rate of undeveloped land being owned by Māori and acknowledging the interests of existing users. It contains a policy intention to work with Māori and regional government to address the water quality and allocation.

In 2018, the government released a policy document on the Māori and Crown relationship with regards to freshwater. It stated that a phased approach would be taken and water quality issues would be addressed before water allocation issues. Policy 10.2 stated that there are three possible options for the Crown and Māori to move forward on freshwater issues:[46]

> 10.2 Option B: find a mechanism to more equitably share the resources over time through a "regulatory" route: in scarce catchments this proposal could require the generation of "headroom" between the total allocated quantum of "use rights" and the sustainable limit in order to give Māori (and other new users) the opportunity to obtain a share of those use rights.

Option A of relying on a resource levy was not considered further because of the Coalition Agreement of the present government. Option B involved an approach where the Courts and Waitangi Tribunal would influence policy outcomes. If Option B is to be pursued, then examining methods by which water allocation law and policy can work to provide that "headroom" between total allocation and sustainable limits will require a careful examination of water allocation law and policy. In 2017, the incoming briefing to the current Minister for the Environment stated that a new allocation system "should include sharper economic incentives" and continues by observing the potential effect on Māori by implementing such instruments:[47]

> 93. Two examples of sharper economic incentives are a cap and trade system, and a price on water or discharges. Note that introducing sharper economic incentives is likely to bring ownership issues to

the foreground, and iwi and hapū rights and interests will need to be addressed in this.

It appears that the Crown reluctance to act on matters regarding water allocation is of benefit to existing permit holders, the majority of which are irrigators. Yet these issues are important to consider when implementing substantive reform in the area of water allocation.

A comparative analysis of New Zealand and Australia

This book compares New Zealand water allocation law and policy with Australian water law and policy. Australia has experienced allocating water to meet environmental and economic needs. It has made significant water law reform since 1994 in response to the Millennium Drought.[48] There are valuable lessons in the extensive Australian experience in water law reform. New Zealand can observe the Australian success and shortfalls during that experience and use those lessons to improve its own water allocation law and policy. Australian water allocation reform included creating a water register, distinguishing bulk water allocation, unbundling of water entitlements and how to regulate water markets.[49] The purpose of the comparison is to consider the lessons from the Australian experience in water law reform that may address New Zealand's water allocation problems. This book argues that changes should be made to New Zealand water allocation law and policy based on the lessons from Australia.

This book contributes to the literature by departing from the traditional accounts of New Zealand water law and policy that focus mainly on the RMA. It contributes to the New Zealand literature on water law and policy by including the impact of privatising irrigation schemes under the Irrigation Schemes Act 1990. A turnaround from divestment in irrigation schemes occurred in May 2011 when New Zealand's National party-led government announced the launch of the Irrigation Acceleration Fund. The Fund would provide an initial public investment in irrigation schemes of $35 million over 5 years to investigate "investment ready" proposals and then increase the amount to $400 million to invest as equity into irrigation schemes.[50] The announcement of the Fund did not address the unresolved issues from the time when irrigation schemes were privatised in 1990. The Fund ended in 2017 when the newly elected Labour government announced a freeze on further investments from the Fund.[51]

A statutory scheme of water allocation was introduced in New Zealand in 1967. The Water and Soil Conservation Act 1967 replaced riparian rights and vested the power to allocate water with the Crown. It established an independent body, the National Water and Soil Conservation Authority, to oversee water allocation. The Act introduced a test for the "beneficial" use of water that would apply to all water users, including government departments wanting water for large-scale projects.[52]

The New Zealand political and economic context is important to understanding the enactment of the RMA and the inclusion of sustainability principles.[53] Sustainability was a concept that was internationally prominent at the time when New Zealand was undertaking extensive environmental reform.[54] In particular, when campaigning for the 1984 general election, Labour's promise to repeal the National Development Act 1979 influenced the mood for widespread environmental reform.[55] The reforms of the 4th Labour government made changes to the economic and social structures of New Zealand. The wide-ranging free-market reforms were seen as somewhat of an experiment by political observers:[56] Under the RMA, government control over resource allocation would be replaced by market-based allocation. In this context the inclusion of sustainability objectives in ensure the protection of natural resources.

Notes

1 Hugh Morris "Cape Town drought: what happens when the city runs out of water?" *The Telegraph* (5 February, 2018).

2 A further 11 cities have been identified as "most likely to run out of drinking water – like Cape Town" including Sao Paulo, Bangalore, Beijing, Cairo, Jakarta, Moscow, Instanbul, Mexico City, London, Tokyo and Miami. See BBC "The 11 cities most likely to run out of drinking water – like Cape Town" (11 February 2018). In 2019, reports emerged that the city of Chennai, India was also running out of water, Kate Wheeling "Chennai, India, is running out of water. Other cities will be next" *Pacific Standard* (24 June 2019).

3 Laurance Boisson de Chazournes and others "Introduction" in Laurance Boisson de Chazournes, and others (eds) *International Law and Freshwater. The Multiple Challenges* (Edward Elgar, Cheltenham, 2013).

4 Quentin R. Grafton "Responding to the 'wicked problem' of water onsecurity" (2017) 31(10) *Water Resour. Manag.* 3023 and Junguo Liu and others "Water scarcity assessments in the past, present, and future" (2017) 5(6) *Earth's Future* 545.

5 Hugh Morris, above n 1. Once the level of water in Cape Town dams falls below 10%, the water is not fit for human consumption and municipal water supply taps will be turned off on a designated "day zero". The availability of water is impacted by its quality.

6 M. Falkenmark, J. Lundquist and C. Widstrand (1989). "Macro-scale water scarcity requires micro-scale approaches: Aspects of vulnerability in semi-arid development" (1989) 13(4) *Natural Resources Forum* 258.

7 Inge de Graaf and others "A global-scale two-layer transient groundwater model: development and application to groundwater depletion" (2017) 102 *Adv. Water Resour.* 53 at 53; and Stephanie L. Castle, Brian F. Thomas, John T. Reager, Matthew Rodell, Sean C. Swenson and James S. Famiglietti "Groundwater

depletion during drought threatens future water security of the Colorado River Basin" (2014) 41(16) *Geophys. Res. Lett.* 5904.

8 J. Van der Gun *Groundwater and Global Change: Trends, Opportunity and Challenges* (UNESCO, Paris, 2012); T. Gleeson, S. Jasechko, E. Luijendijk, M. Cardenas "The global volume and distribution of modern groundwater" (2016) 9(2) *Nat. Geosci.* 161; and G.M. Zuppi "The Groundwater Challenge" in Corrado Clini, Ignazio Musu and Maria Lodovica Gullino (eds) *Sustainable Development and Environmental Management. Experiences and Case Studies* (Springer, Netherlands, 2008) at 52.

9 The material in this paragraph is drawn from Frank R. Rijsberman, "Water scarcity: fact or fiction?" (2006) 80(1) *Agricultural Water Management* 5 at 5 where the author poses the question of "What is water scarcity?".

10 See Water Act 2007 (Cth) and the Murray-Darling Basin Plan, which has a targeted reduction of water extractions in the Murray-Darling Basin prompted in part by concerns about over-extraction and physical water scarcity.

11 See National Policy Statement Freshwater Management 2014 (revised 2017), which has put in place targets for regional councils to stop over-allocation.

12 At 3.

13 United Nations *Introduction and Proposed Goals and Targets on Sustainable Development for the Post 2015 Development Agenda* (2014); Théa Bounfour "International Water Law and the Sustainable Development Goals" (2016) 46(6) EPIL 380.

14 Anik Bhaduri and others "Achieving sustainable development goals from a water perspective" (2016) 4 *Front. Environ. Sci.* 64.

15 "United Nations Water" is a United Nations inter-agency department for freshwater-related issues established in 2003 by the United Nations High Level Committee on Programmes.

16 United Nations *High Level Plan on Water* (United Nations, High Level Panel on Water, 2016).

17 D. Vanham and others "Physical water scarcity metrics for monitoring progress towards SDG target 6.4: An evaluation of indicator 6.4.2 'Level of water stress'" (2018) 613 *Sci. Total Environ.* 218.

18 United Nations, above n 32, at 4.

19 At 6.

20 Naho Mirumachi "Water and Sustainable Development" in Michael Redclift & Delyse Springett *Routledge International Handbook of Sustainable Development* (Routledge, London, 2015) at 137.

21 Robert Wilkinson "The Water-Energy Nexus Methodologies, Challenges and Opportunities" in Douglas S. Kenney & Robert Wilkinson (eds) *The Water-Energy Nexus in the American West* (Edward Elgar, Cheltenham, 2011) at 5.

22 Xuexia Jia and others "Analyzing the energy consumption, GHG emission, and cost of seawater desalination in China" (2019) 12(463) *Energies* 1.

23 Wilkinson, above n 38, at 7.

24 At 7.

25 Douglas E. Fisher *The Law and Governance of Water Resources: The Challenge of Sustainability* (Edward Elgar, Cheltenham, 2009) for an analysis of sustainability in Australian water law and policy.

26 Ganesh Keremane, Jennifer McKay and Zhifang Wu "Achieving Ecologically Sustainable Development in Multi-level Water Governance Regimes: the Case of the Murray Darling Basin" 211 in Michael Kidd, Loretta Feris and Tumai

Murombo (eds) *Water and the Law towards Sustainability* (Edward Elgar, Cheltenham, 2014).

27 Above.

28 Hon Simon Upton, "Stace Hammond Grace Lecture: Purpose and Principle in the Resource Management Act" (1995) 3 *Waikato L. Rev.* 17; Caroline Miller *Implementing Sustainability. The New Zealand Experience* (Routledge, New York, 2011); Bret C. Birdsong "Adjudicating Sustainability. New Zealand's Environment Court and the Resource Management Act" (2002) 29(1) *Ecology L.Q.* 1 and Nicola Wheen "The Resource Management Act 1991: A Greener Law for Water" (1997) 1 *NZJ Envtl. L.* 165.

29 Trevor Daya-Winterbottom "Sustainability, Governance and Water Management in New Zealand" in Michael Kidd, Loretta Feris and Tumai Murombo (eds) *Water and the Law towards Sustainability* (Edward Elgar, Cheltenham, 2014).

30 Hon Simon Upton "Stace Hammond Grace Lecture: Purpose and Principle in the Resource Management Act" (1995) 3 *Waikato L. Rev.* 17; Caroline Miller *Implementing Sustainability. The New Zealand Experience* (Routledge, New York, 2011); Geoffrey Palmer *Environmental Politics. A Greenprint for New Zealand* (John McIndoe, Dunedin, 1990); and Nicola Wheen "A Natural Flow – A History of Water Law in New Zealand" (1997) 9(1) *Otago L. Rev.* 71.

31 Ministry for the Environment *The State of New Zealand's Environment 1997* (Ministry for the Environment, Wellington, 1997) provides an overview of the Resource Management Law Reform Project; and Nicola Wheen "The Resource Management Act 1991: A Greener Law for Water" (1997) 1 NZJ Envtl. L. 165.

32 Geoffrey Palmer "The Resource Management Act – How we got it and what changes are being made to it" (paper presented to Address to Resource Management Law Association 27 September 2013, New Plymouth, 2013). The Land and Water Forum has undertaken significant policy work which includes identifying problems with water quality and allocation under the RMA. New Zealand; Land and Water Forum *Terms of Reference for Land and Water Forum Project* (Land and Water Forum, Wellington, 2009); Land and Water Forum *Report of the Land and Water Forum: A Fresh Start for Fresh Water* (Land and Water Trust, Wellington, 2010); Land and Water Forum Second *Report of the Land and Water Forum. Setting Limits for Water Quality and Quantity* (Land and Water Trust, Wellington, 2012); Land and Water Forum *Third Report of the Land and Water Forum: Managing Water Quality and Allocating Water* (Land and Water Trust, Wellington, 2012); Land and Water Forum *Fourth Report of the Land and Water Forum* (Land and Water Forum Trust, Wellington, 2015).

33 National policy was only promulgated in 2011. See National Policy Statement for Freshwater Management 2011. Revised in 2014 and reviewed in 2017.

34 Establishing regional plans is one of the "functions" of regional councils under section 30 of the RMA. A key distinction in the New Zealand context is that a "function" does not confer a legal obligation to create the regional plan. District plans must have regard to regional policy and not be inconsistent with National Policy Statements. See Resource Management Act, section 73(4).

35 However, it is important to acknowledge that there was no statutory obligation for the government to create a National Policy Statement for water under the RMA. Establishing National Policy Statements is also expressed as one of the "functions" of regional councils under section 24(a) of the RMA. The Minister for the Environment may recommend the issue of a National Policy Statement subject to the process in section 52 of the Act.

36   *Fleetwing Farms Ltd v Marlborough District Council* [1997] 3 NZLR 257 (CA).

37   New Zealand Government *Briefing to the Incoming Ministers – Environment and Climate Change* (Ministry for the Environment, Wellington, 2017) at 11. See also the extensive policy work undertaken by the Land and Water Forum in their four reports at n 3 above. Sarah Boone and Stephen Fragaszy "Emerging Scarcity and Emerging Commons: Water Management Groups and Groundwater Governance In Aotearoa New Zealand" (2018) 11(3) Water Alternatives 795.

38   "allocation, n." OED Online. Oxford University Press, June 2019. Web. 16 July 2019.

39   Nicola Wheen "A Natural Flow – A History of Water Law in New Zealand" above, n 1, at 75.

40   At 72.

41   At 72.

42   Jacinta Ruru *The Legal Voice of Māori in Freshwater Governance. A Literature Review.* (Landcare Research, 2009).

43   Elizabeth Macpherson and others "Lessons from Australian Water Reforms: indigenous and Environmental Values in Market-Based Water Regulation" in Cameron Holley and Darren Sinclair (eds) *Reforming Water Law and Governance* (Springer, Singapore, 2018).

44   Ministry for the Environment and Māori Crown Relations Unit. *Shared Interests in Freshwater: A New Approach to the Crown/Māori Relationship for Freshwater.* (Ministry for the Environment and Māori Crown Relations Unit, Wellington, 2018).

45   Cabinet Paper "A New Approach to Crown/Maori Relationship for Freshwater" (3 July 2018) CAB 18-00032.

46   Ministry for the Environment and Māori Crown Relations Unit, above n 24 at 39.

47   Ministry for the Environment *Briefing for the Incoming Minister for the Environment. Water Issues.* (Ministry for the Environment, Wellington, 2017) at 19.

48   The Council of Australian Government (COAG) *COAG Water Reform Framework 1994 – Attachment A: Water Resource Policy* (Communique, 25 February 1994); Productivity Commission *Impact of Competition Policy Reforms on Rural and Regional Australia*, Report No. 8 (Productivity Commission, Canberra, 1999); National Water Initiative 2004; Water Act 2007 (Cth); Cameron Holley and Darren Sinclair (eds) *Reforming Water Law and Governance. From Stagnation to Innovation in Australia* (Springer, Singapore, 2018); John Quiggin, Thilak Mallawaarachchi and Sarah Chambers (eds) *Water Policy Reform, Lessons in Sustainability from the Murray Darling Basin* (Edward Elgar, Cheltenham, 2012); Murray-Darling Basin Authority *Guide to the Proposed Basin Plan* (MDBA, Canberra, 2010); Daniel Connell and Quentin Grafton "Planning for water security in the Murray-Darling Basin" (2008) 3(1) Public Policy 67; and Australian Government, Murray-Darling Basin Authority A Path to Water Reform. Timeline of Water Resource Management in the Murray-Darling Basin (Murray-Darling Basin Authority, Canberra, n.d.).

49   Water Act 2007 (Cth).

50   David Carter "Budget 2011: Lifting investment in irrigation" *New Zealand Government* (9 May 2011) – Press Release.

51   Labour, New Zealand First, New Zealand Labour Party & New Zealand First Coalition Agreement 52nd Parliament (Labour, New Zealand First, Wellington, 2017).

52 *Keam v Minister of Works and Development* [1982] 1 NZLR 319. *Stanley v South Canterbury Catchment Board* (1971) Planning Tribunal 463,68.

53 Miller, above n 1; Palmer, above n 33 at 19 notes the political context of the RMA is an important part of understanding the main policy drivers of the legislation: "As such it is impossible to understand the RMA without understanding the reform context from which it emerged".

54 The fourth Labour government committed New Zealand to a nuclear free zone as a signatory of the South Pacific Nuclear Free Zone Treaty 1985 and New Zealand Nuclear Free Zone, Disarmament, and Arms Control Act 1987.

55 Geoffrey Palmer "The Resource Management Act – How we got it and what changes are being made to it" (paper presented to Address the Resource Management Law Association 27 September 2013, New Plymouth, 2013).

56 Jane Kelsey, *The New Zealand Experiment. A World Model for Structural Adjustment* (Auckland University Press with Bridget Williams Books, Auckland, 1995) at 2.

2 The water allocation policy gap 1991–2011

Introduction

This chapter critically evaluates the New Zealand water allocation framework under the Resource Management Act (RMA).[1] The purpose of the framework is to allocate natural resources, including water, based on a tiered hierarchy of policies and plans at the national and regional level.[2] At the top of the hierarchy central government was "expected", but not obliged, to prepare national policies in the form of National Policy Statements.[3] However, a National Policy Statement for freshwater management was not prepared until 2011.[4] This oversight resulted in what can be termed a water allocation policy gap that existed from 1991, the date the RMA was enacted, to 2011. In addition, the policy gap was exacerbated because at the local government levels of the framework, the regional councils responsible for regional plans and who relied on the provisions of the RMA when embarking upon water allocation planning, either did not prepare them or failed to provide adequate guidance on water allocation.[5] These policy gaps at both the national and regional level form the context for water allocation in New Zealand under the RMA.[6]

A consequence of the New Zealand government and regional council's failure to implement a comprehensive water allocation policy is that the precedent set in *Fleetwing Farms Ltd v Marlborough District Council*[7] has become the default position. This precedent, therefore, forms an integral part of the regional council water allocation consent process. However, as will be shown in this chapter, a problem with this precedent is that it is inherently unsustainable in that it gives "preference to current rather than potential users" of water.[8] In addition, despite the development of a national policy for water allocation in 2011, the precedent continues to apply when determining a priority between competing water allocation applications.[9]

This chapter introduces the national water policy gap, how it originated and its consequences for water allocation in New Zealand from 1991 until

2011. It describes how some regions reached water allocation limits and the details of the absence of long-term hydrological data. The chapter then provides an account of the water allocation provisions and case law under the RMA. It includes an account of relevant water allocation rules and policies in regional plans and the application of the "first in, first served" precedent.[10]

Water policy – a gap in national guidance on water allocation policies

Water allocation limits

Water allocation limits in New Zealand are set by regional councils within regional plans under section 30 of the RMA.[11] As described in Chapter 1, water allocation is the process of determining the amount of water (surface or groundwater) that can be allocated from a water resource. Surface water allocation from rivers and lakes is based on environmental flow regimes which determine how much water can be allocated. The amount of water in a water body that can be allocated for take or use is also referred to as the allocable flow.[12] The setting of environmental flows involves the consideration of several factors under the RMA.[13] Setting minimum flows relies upon information about the volume of water abstracted and monitoring data enables regional councils to predict how a catchment may respond to changes in abstraction.[14]

Government policy documents on water allocation during the 2000s focused on how to manage increasing demand for water.[15] Full allocation and over-allocation were recognised as issues in specific regions.[16] Consultation on the Sustainable Water Program of Action (SWOPA) identified problems with the setting of environmental flows, such as not all water bodies having environmental flow limits.[17]

SWOPA policy initiatives from 2003 until 2008 identified "gaps in current policy" and were only able to develop some "soft options" in the form of policy advice to regional councils.[18] The SWOPA "failed"[19] as it was unsuccessful in implementing a National Policy Statement for freshwater or a National Environmental Standard for establishing water flows.[20] A proposed National Environmental Standard for setting environmental flows was notified in 2008 but did not proceed further to being implemented.[21] The RMA does not include legal consequences for governments or government departments failing to prepare national direction.

Effectively, the SWOPA failed to be implemented because of a change of government in 2008, when the National party won the 2008 general election. The incoming briefing for the Minister stated the problems with water allocation.[22] The SWOPA lost momentum and instead an agreement was developed between environmental groups and non-government organisations interested in water, the Sustainable Land Use Forum.[23] This Forum secured the support of the newly elected National-led government, which led to the formation of the Land and Water Forum.[24] By this time the National-led government had moved onto a new policy programme to address the water policy gap, "A New Start for Freshwater".[25]

The lack of historical hydrological information

During the time the RMA has been in force, long-term hydrological data collection occurred irregularly.[26] The lack of systematic data collection should have been addressed by the implementation of the Resource Management (Measurement and Reporting of Water Takes) Regulations 2010.[27] However, evidence shows that the implementation of the 2010 Regulations fell short in some regions. For example, a lack of monitoring of water takes was reported in the Canterbury region. This region had the highest number of water take consents because of the conversion of pastures to dairy farming increasing demand for irrigation.[28] Lack of data and the absence of monitoring meant that potentially millions of litres of water had been taken illegally.[29] There have been "serious breaches" of water permits.[30] A lack of regional council data collection on actual use was confirmed in national hydrological data reporting. In their first joint report on freshwater statistics based on regional council hydrological data, the Ministry for the Environment and Statistics New Zealand[31] reported that although over half of water allocation consents were for irrigation, there was a lack of data on water use.[32] The implications of the lack of data collection for water allocation policy and planning is that regional councils are hampered by not knowing how much water is taken under each consent.

More recently, New Zealand's water allocation, and in particular the lack of data on water takes, has gained international attention. For example, in its 2015 environmental performance report on New Zealand, the Organisation for Economic Co-operation and Development (OECD) pointed out the lack of groundwater information, stating: "No mapping exercise has been done to identify areas where scarcity of groundwater is becoming a problem".[33] Concerns were also expressed in the 2017 OECD report where it was noted that "rising freshwater pollution and scarcity in some areas" was one of the environmental challenges faced by New Zealand.[34] The 2017 report also recommended the use of economic instruments to manage water quantity and quality.[35] Recommendations relevant to water allocation included introducing "volumetric pricing to recover costs of water management and reflect environment impacts … and expand water markets";[36] and "experiment with natural capital accounting to provide a basis for valuing water resources and freshwater ecosystems, and quantifying costs and benefits of freshwater policy and management decisions".[37] The points in relation to water markets have also been stated in more recent New Zealand policy from the Land and Water Forum, which is discussed in more detail in the next chapter. It is important to recognise that introducing water markets would require the collection of historical water take information, not just information about how much water was consented to be taken. The Resource Management (Measurement and Reporting of Water Takes) Regulations 2010 need to be implemented and enforced successfully before water markets could be considered for New Zealand.

Statutory framework – water allocation under the RMA

As stated above, the absence of a national water allocation policy gap between 1991 and 2011 contributed to the water allocation problems that exist in New Zealand during this period. At the central government level, the failure to create national policy "has left the RMA operating in a partial vacuum".[38] This policy gap is an example of the "failure of the RMA".[39]

The provisions within the RMA were intended to establish a regulatory framework for resource allocation, including water allocation. The following analysis of statutory provisions relevant to water allocation shows that the RMA was not designed to regulate a market-based system of water allocation. This point has great significance in light of any proposal to introduce market-based allocation in the future, as is discussed in the next chapter. The RMA provides the regulatory basis for various bodies that have administrative, judicial and decision-making roles relevant to water allocation.[40] This section provides an account of the functions, powers and duties of central and local government under the relevant provisions of the RMA. Each section contributes to the understanding that the RMA does not include any foundation for market-based water allocation in its current form. At times this point is secondary to the perception that the RMA has failed to be implemented as intended.

How does the RMA 'allocate' water?

The functions, powers and duties of central government

The provisions of the RMA establish a hierarchical structure of policy guidance for resource allocation at the national and regional level. Within this regulatory framework, the responsibility for resource allocation is split between local and central government (as stated in Part 4 of the Act) with devolution of power to the regional level.[41] The Ministry for the Environment (which administers the RMA) is primarily responsible for developing national environmental policy. Adding complexity to matters is that in addition to the Minister for the Environment, the Ministers of Conservation and Aquaculture also have roles in policy development. For example, the Minister of Conservation is responsible for the preparation of the New Zealand coastal policy statement under section 57 of the RMA. The Environmental Protection Authority and the Environment Court have decision-making roles.[42] For example, The Environmental Protection Authority has jurisdiction over projects of "national significance".[43] The Environment Court can hold the first judicial hearing relating to Regional Plans and Policy Statements, resource consent applications, enforcement proceedings and declarations.[44]

The RMA states the statutory process for setting "national direction" in the promulgation of National Environmental Standards, National Policy Statements and the New Zealand Coastal Policy Statement.[45] RMA amendments to set "national direction" reflect the ongoing tension between balancing the needs of development while at the same time protecting the environment.[46] For example, section 46A of the RMA was amended in 2017 which allowed a "single consultation process" when developing "national direction" concurrently for the same environmental issue.[47] The amendment means that National Policy Statements and National Environmental Standards can be developed at the same time without requiring separate processes for public consultation. The change should "increase flexibility in the development of national direction".[48] Once the subject of "national direction" is determined, the Minister may either follow the process in the RMA (sections 47 to 51) that sets out a board of inquiry process, or follow the method described in section 46A(4).[49] Section 46A(4) outlines the steps required to prepare national direction. This includes providing public notice of the proposed national direction and the reason "why the Minister considers that the proposed national direction is consistent with the purpose of the Act".[50]

The Minister may appoint a board of inquiry to "inquire into, and report on, the proposed national direction".[51] The Minister has the power to set the "terms of reference" for the board of inquiry.[52] The Minister also has the power to suspend the board of inquiry "at any time" subject to providing public notice for the reasons for the suspension.[53] The purpose of the public notification phase is to invite submissions on the proposed national direction.[54] The role of the board of inquiry is to provide recommendations for the Minister on the proposed national direction.[55]

In addition to these changes to the setting of national direction, the 2017 Amendments also introduced provisions to allow national planning templates for regional planning.[56] However, not all of these changes to setting national direction are welcomed by commentators. For example, Palmer is critical of amendments which dilute features of the RMA planning process, resulting in increased central government control over planning and encroaching on regional planning.[57] In the past, without adequate national direction, "New Zealand overshot the mark in terms of decentralization and local decision making".[58] The "balance of power" between the central government and regional government "did not come into fruition as planned".[59] Palmer's analysis attributes the failure of local government to adequately plan, as follows: "Too often local government did not appreciate its duties under the Act and there was too much political interference".[60] It remains to be seen whether the latest changes to the setting of national direction are able to address the pressing issues facing New Zealand water allocation. A point to note is that there remain no legal consequences for government departments failing to prepare national direction under the RMA.

The functions, powers and duties of regional government

The "functions" of regional councils are preparing plans with policies and objectives that further the purpose of the RMA.[61] These statutory "functions" do not confer an obligation to create a regional plan.[62] Regional plans may address any of the functions stated in section 30.[63] Section 30(1)(e) to (fa) state regional councils may specify maximum or minimum flows and prepare rules for taking or using water. The water allocation function of regional councils was amended in 2005 within a broader context to streamline environmental planning.[64] These sections provide regional councils with the means to develop rules in regional plans to allocate water.[65] Examples illustrating how rules may be formulated in regional plans are discussed later in this chapter.

Regional councils determine how much water can be allocated by setting limits on the amount of water that can be taken from a body of water.[66] Environmental flow limits are placed on surface water bodies. In 2006, the Ministry for the Environment identified problems with the minimum flows, including that there were still some freshwater bodies for which "no specific environmental flows and water levels have been determined".[67]

Regional plans do not "pre-allocate" water to specific uses.[68] One exception to this is the Waitaki Regional Water Allocation Plan. The plan is not the norm; it is an example of ad hoc central government intervention in regional water allocation planning.[69] The central government intervention in the Waitaki region occurred through the establishment of a statutory Water Allocation Board to "develop and approve a regional plan for water allocation".[70] Reasons for the intervention were justified on the seriousness of water allocation that would "sacrifice the interest of the people of the Waitaki catchment".[71] A further example of ad hoc or "unprecedented" government intervention was the appointment of Commissioners in the Canterbury region, described later in this chapter.[72]

One of the features of the water allocation plan in Waitaki is the use of sector-based allocation. Sector-based allocation in the Waitaki region reduces "reliance" on the "first in, first served" method of water allocation.[73] Sector-based water allocation is described as *"planned* allocation".[74] The downside of *"planned* allocation" is how to determine which sector gains an initial allocation and the volume of water to be allocated to each sector.[75] The positive feature of *"planned* allocation" is that priorities for water allocation can be determined with a greater level of "sophistication" by varying sector allocations across seasonal demand patterns.[76] Central government intervention in the Waitaki region raises the question of why the method of *"planned* allocation" for water sectors cannot be implemented in other regions.

The preparation of regional plans requires a cost-benefit evaluation to be undertaken. The evaluation report forms part of the public consultation required under the RMA and is an important step in the plan making process.[77] It is required under section 32 of the RMA for a proposed plan, plan change or variation in order to assess how the proposal meets the overall objective of the RMA. The evaluation should also consider alternatives to address the particular environmental issue and the efficiency of each option.[78] The cost-benefit analysis includes a consideration of financial and non-financial values.[79] The resulting evaluation report should "identify and assess the benefits and costs of the environmental, economic, social, and cultural effects" including economic growth and employment.[80] Examples of costs include administrative costs, compliance costs, broader economic costs, social costs and environmental costs.[81] Amendments to section 32 requirements in 2013 added the consideration of "economic growth" and "employment".[82] However, such changes have been criticised as going too far in attempting to follow central government's business and economic growth agenda.[83]

Part 3 of the RMA details statutory restrictions on the use of resources. Section 14 details the restrictions relating to the take and use of water, which specifically allows the "take" and "use" of water for personal use.[84] Section 14(3)(b) allows water to be taken for the "reasonable" needs of people for "domestic needs" or "of a person's animals for drinking water". All other water allocations are restricted and subject to provisions in regional plans, which may require a resource consent.[85] Other statutory control over water takes in the RMA includes regional council power to issue a "Water Shortage Direction" for up to 14 days for any water body.[86]

From a legal perspective, there is no inherent right to access water and the granting of water permit is a lifting of this general restriction to take water from the commons. Section 122(1) of the RMA states a resource consent is "neither real nor personal property". However, there are exceptions to this general rule. Under section 122(2), there are three situations where the resource consent may vest as personal property. The first is when the resource consent holder dies and the resource consent vests with the "personal representative of the holder". The second is if the consent holder becomes bankrupt and the resource consent is vested with the Official Assignee "as if it were personal property". The third situation is where the resource consent is listed as property under the Protection of Personal Properties and Property Rights Act 1998. These situations show that there are a number of practical situations where a resource consent is clearly recognised as property.

The RMA recognises property in a resource consent as "goods" in section 122(4) for the purpose of registration as collateral under the Personal Property Securities Act 1999. This section is different from the situations addressed under section 122(3) because it also allows a charge to be registered against the resource consent. That means that water permits can be provided as security for loans and the charge over the water permit can be registered as "goods". Effectively, water permit holders can deal with the permit as if it is property and there is a clear legal basis for them to do so. Barton supports the view that resource consents have been interpreted as a type of property by the Courts, but questions the correctness of the use of property-related concepts.[87] There is concern that the application of property-related concepts to legal issues relating to resource consents may have gone too far. It is important to remember the general rule in section 122(1) does not support that view that a resource consent provides the consent holder with property. These concerns are discussed in more detail in the case law analysed in this chapter. It is clear that under the RMA, water permits cannot be owned or traded as they are in other jurisdictions operating water allocation via market-based regulation.

The transfer of water permits under the RMA

The rules for water transfers in regional plans must comply with the administrative requirements of section 136 of the RMA. Section 136 allows for the permanent or temporary transfer of a water permit to another person or site within the same catchment or aquifer, with the subject complying with the relevant regional plan.[88] When transfers occur, regional plans may require notification details of transfers to be provided to the regional council such as location, duration, volume transferred and details of parties involved in the transfer.[89] New Zealand does not have central or regional water registers. Regional councils may consider themselves as repositories of water information, but not legal registers. Each regional council may stipulate its own rules for water transfers, which can vary. For example, in some regional plans, a water transfer may only occur if a portion of the allocation is surrendered in over-allocated catchments.[90] Or, there may be a requirement for a transfer to be efficient.[91] Section 136 does not require the collection of information regarding the agreed price of the transfer.

Despite the lack of formal water registers in New Zealand, case law illustrates regional councils have an important role in accurately recording information regarding water transfers. A case where negligence by the regional council was alleged was *The Favourite Ltd v Vavasour*.[92] Vavasour held a water permit for vineyard irrigation. When Vavasour transferred the water permit to another party, The Favourite Ltd argued that the water permit was incorrectly transferred. Vavasour, The Favourite Limited and the third party had private dealings regarding the water permit. The Favourite Limited unsuccessfully argued the regional council had a duty of care in transferring the new water permit holder's details into its records because it disputed the validity of the transfer.

The Court held that a duty of care was not owed by the regional council in this case because it was unaware of the private dealings between the parties. In these situations, the role of the regional council was more like a "postbox":[93]

> Section 136 therefore makes a distinction between the situation where the holder is transferring a permit to an owner or occupier and that where the holder is transferring the permit to another person on another site. Obviously (see s 136 (4)), the council does have a role in the second situation. It does not flow from that that there is any obligation on the council to determine which category a purported transfer is in. Rather, in terms of s 136(2)(a) the council is, as Mr Radich, put it, a postbox. The council receives the transfer and notes its register accordingly. That the council has no active role is supported by s 136(3) which indicates that the transfer is ineffective until "received" by the relevant consent authority.

This case confirmed that the role of regional councils is to receive and record the transfer, subject to the transfer being allowed in the regional plan.

However, negligence by a regional council in the recording of water permit information is possible. Negligence by the regional council was found in *Altimarloch Joint Venture Ltd v Moorhouse*, where the Marlborough District Council was found liable in the High Court of incorrectly providing water permit information in a Land Information Memorandum (LIM).[94] The water permit information recorded in the LIM recorded a lower volume of water than the volume Altimarloch Joint Ventures Limited believed they were acquiring. It relied upon the information in the LIM when deciding to purchase the property and associated water permits. Damages of $400,000 were awarded in the High Court. The value of damages was quantified on the financial loss to the plaintiffs as a result of relying upon incorrect water permit information supplied in the LIM.[95] The Court of Appeal dismissed an appeal by the regional council and maintained the equal apportionment of damages between the vendors and the regional council.[96] The Court of Appeal also confirmed the duty of care owed by the regional council to the purchasers when providing a LIM under section 44A of the Local Government Official Information and Meetings Act 1987. On appeal, the Supreme Court also confirmed that a duty is imposed on regional councils to provide the correct information. The Supreme Court's decision focused on the issues of how to determine the appropriate apportionment of liability between the regional council and other parties involved in the case. It held that damages were based on the cost of finding another source of water, not the difference in the value of the property purchased based on the diminution of the water permits.[97]

This case shows the recording of water permit information is subject to a high standard of care. Water permits are valuable assets. The value of water permits means that mistakes can be costly to remedy. Regional councils may be required to pay costs if negligence is proven on their behalf and they may not appreciate that they are the holders of information about increasingly valuable water assets. The issues described in this section are exacerbated by New Zealand not having a water register. In light of the duty of care imposed on regional councils to maintain correct records, a national water register, similar to the water register in Australia, should be considered. The feasibility of implementing a national water register will be discussed later in this book.

Setting minimum flows – from national direction to regional responsibility

Regional councils can create rules to specify minimum flows (which are based on the quantity, level or flow of water) under section 30(1)(e) of the RMA. This section preserves the provisions for fixing minimum water flows originally contained in the Water and Soil Conservation Act 1967.[98] A significant change to set minimum flows under the RMA was the devolution of this function to regional councils. Before the RMA, the National Water and Soil Conservation Authority set minimum flow levels. It was required to consult "all interested bodies and persons known to the Authority", but there was no right of appeal to the Authority's decision on minimum flow levels.[99] The most noteworthy cases relating to the setting of minimum flows under the Water and Soil Conservation Act 1967 and the RMA are discussed below. These cases show a shift in factors that are taken into consideration when setting minimum flows.

Electricity Corporation of New Zealand Ltd v Manawatu-Wanganui Regional Council

This case provides an insight into the relevant factors considered when setting minimum flow levels under the Water and Soil Conservation Act 1967. This case dealt with the question of whether the minimum flow set for the Wanganui River was fixed at an appropriate level by the regional water board. It is a significant case because of its timing, context and precedent value.[100] The National Water and Soil Conservation Authority was abolished and the decision to set the minimum flow lay with the Planning Tribunal.

On 1 November 1983, the National Water and Soil Conservation Authority fixed the minimum flow of the river for five years, expiring on 31 October 1988 under the Water and Soil Conservation Act 1967.

In March 1987, the catchment board again began the process to fix the minimum flow. A call for public submissions was made in February 1988. Twelve hundred and fifty submissions were received from around New Zealand. A month later, on 31 March 1988, the Water and Soil Conservation Authority was abolished. The Rangitikei-Wanganui Catchment Board became responsible for setting the minimum flows on the Wanganui River.

When the catchment board fixed the minimum flow on 18 October 1988, unlike the Authority, its decision was subject to appeal. The right of appeal was emphasised in the case as there was no precedent for setting minimum flows.[101]

The Planning Tribunal was faced with a mammoth task of setting the minimum flow without the benefit of precedents or statutory criteria.[102] Following an extensive assessment, the Court found that the balancing test applied:[103]

> It was generally accepted by the parties that in setting minimum acceptable flow, the decision-maker is to follow a process similar to that approved in Keam's case of evaluating and balancing all the relevant considerations.

In determining an acceptable flow, future potential uses were not trumped by existing uses.[104] The Court found that on balance the minimum flow that had been set could be adjusted at some points. This case confirmed that arguments based on legitimate expectation were not suitable for fixing minimum flow and that the ability to be granted a water consent was a privilege and not a right. On appeal, the High Court affirmed the Planning Tribunal's decision.

The setting of minimum flows under the RMA

Amendments to the Otago Regional Council Water Plan

Under the RMA, minimum flows are subject to appeal. One of the earliest cases involved the setting of flows in the Otago Regional Water Plan. The plan was appealed on issues relating to minimum flow, mining rights and setting supplementary flow.[105] In these cases, the reduction in minimum flow was considered to "have the most immediate and critical importance to the irrigation groups before the Court".[106] The setting of minimum flows, in this case, should be distinguished on its facts because of the existence and effect of mining privileges as deemed permits under the RMA, which may not exist or affect the setting of minimum flows in other regions.

The Otago Regional Water Plan has been revised since it became operative on 1 January 2004.[107] The changes focused on improving the connections between groundwater and surface water and addressed governance and water quality issues.[108]

The setting of minimum flows by the Waikato Regional Council

Another example of setting minimum flows under the RMA is Waikato Regional Council's Variation 6 to its regional plan. Variation 6 included a range of changes to improve water allocation including the setting of minimum flows and improving environmental education. The issue before the Court was whether the minimum flow at points of the Waikato River was fixed at an appropriate level.[109]

In setting the minimum flow for the Waikato River, the Environment Court considered a number of statutory requirements. Section 66(2) of the RMA required the regional council to take into consideration any proposed policy statements and relevant plans under other Acts. Section 67(3) required giving effect to any National Policy Statements. At this point, the relevant Acts included the Waikato-Tainui Raupatu Claims (Waikato River) Settlement Act 2010, including Schedule 2 containing the Vision and Strategy for the Waikato River; and the Ngati Tuwharetoa, Raukawa, and Te Arawa River Iwi Waikato River Act 2010. This Act was part of a settlement process with the tribes of the Waikato region.[110] The relevant National Policy Statements were the National Policy Statement for Renewable Electricity Generation 2011 and the National Policy Statement for Freshwater Management 2011.

The Court found against Waikato Regional Council in finding that there should be an increase in the allocable flow above Karapiro. Horticulture water users (represented by Horticulture New Zealand) had concerns about maintaining access to water at times when minimum flows were reached and sought priority in Variation 6 addressing minimum flows and water allocation. The key argument was that horticultural crops were less likely to be tolerant of drought conditions, which meant their water take should be prioritised. However, the arguments for priority were not accepted.

The setting of a minimum flow can vary across catchments. Each regional council can determine the method and minimum flow for different water bodies. The challenge to the Waikato Regional Council illustrated the lack of precedent for setting minimum flow levels under the RMA.

Minor and major water allocation in regional plans

Regional plans should include specific rules on water allocation such as rules for setting minimum flows as explained above. This section examines the other objectives, policies and rules that determine how water is allocated in regional plans. For the purpose of discussion in this section, the rules for water allocation in regional plans are categorised into those for minor and major water takes.[111] A comparable concept is that of *"planned* allocation" across different water sectors as has been implemented in the Waitaki region.[112] In the New Zealand context, it is the major water takes that are a more significant part of the water allocation story and deserve greater attention. The themes that emerge from analysing regional plans are the variation in water allocation policies and the lack of comprehensive rules for major water takes such as irrigation or municipal water supply.[113] Some regions may not have prepared water allocation rules to prevent over-allocation.[114]

Minor water takes include those takes permitted by regional plans and the RMA. Domestic water takes are one category of water take. However, minor water takes are not a significant part of water allocation in New Zealand.[115] Domestic water takes are allowed under section 14(3)(b) of the RMA for an "individual's reasonable domestic needs". Domestic takes do not require a water allocation application to be made. Regional plans have addressed domestic water takes by defining the domestic water needs in section 14(3) (b) in a number of ways. This includes varying interpretation of "reasonable" needs for domestic water use. For example, Horizons Regional Council has placed a daily limit of 300 litres per person for domestic water takes.[116] In comparison, other regional councils have domestic water takes based on property or landholding, rather than a personal limit.[117] A further example of a minor take is dairy-shed washdown water. Previously, dairy-shed washdown water was not subject to the level of control and information collection that is now being included in some regional plans.[118]

Major water takes and irrigation in regional plans

Some water takes which are actually minor in nature have a higher profile than the cumulative effect of water takes that are from a major water use sector.[119] Regional council statistics show that water for irrigation accounts for over half of all consented water allocations in New Zealand.[120] The lack of actual data on water takes affected the perception of sector-based water use. In 2018, the Auditor General audited how freshwater is measured and recommended that central government must guide regional councils towards the more efficient use of water.[121] Water for irrigation has been a problem in some regions such as the Manawatu-Whanganui and Canterbury regions. The following analysis draws upon these examples of regional plans that address water takes with reference to irrigation.

Horizons Regional Council One Plan

The Horizons Regional Council Regional Plan, One Plan, stated that Horizons Region has usually maintained adequate access to water for people's needs but that water still needs to be managed in response to dairy farming intensification.[122] The intensification of agriculture was linked to both water quality and water quantity in the quote above. Water quality was a particular issue in the region.[123] The Horizons Regional Council had a policy of "reasonable and justifiable need for water" that must be met by applicants for certain water uses in Policy 5–12. These rules linked the justification for water use to the characteristics of the soil. The basis for the regional council decision includes objective scientific measures and estimates. Objective scientific measures may assist in preventing speculative applications for irrigation water that is beyond the applicant's reasonable needs. Further issues arose with the One Plan in 2017 when it was alleged that the Horizons Regional Council failed to implement water quality rules 14.2 and 14.4.[124] The decision set a precedent for all regional councils to fully implement regional plan rules.

Environment Canterbury

Water allocation in Canterbury is a practical example of the failure of the RMA. Problems with Canterbury's regional planning for water allocation were identified in 2007.[125] Environment Canterbury had not developed a regional water allocation plan under the RMA. Instead, Canterbury had "a long history of experimenting with CG [collaborative governance] approaches as a complement to its traditional regulatory role".[126] In theory, collaborative governance provides more "flexible and cheaper regulations", can bring together divided communities, "offers environmental outcomes that are as good as or better than top down regulation" and can expand democratic participation.[127] However, the experience in Canterbury challenges these theoretical assertions.

The 2010 Government Review of Environment Canterbury found "a significant gap, characterised as 'enormous and unprecedented', between what needs to be done in Canterbury to appropriately manage water and ECan's ability to do so".[128] One of the key omissions was that Environment Canterbury did not have a statutory plan for water management.[129]

The reason for the lack of progress was stated in another research paper, published before the Review Group Report, identifying a policy gridlock on water modelling.[130] The gridlock involved perceived differences between water allocation models. "The centre of Canterbury's struggle over water management is the science that maps the hydrological characteristics of the region".[131] On the one hand, the "Aqualinc" model "supports the continuing withdrawal of groundwater".[132] On the other hand, Environment Canterbury, environmentalists and urban residents tended to find greater validity in the computer modelling, i.e. the "bathtub" model. The "bathtub" model supported the idea that water takes in one aquifer impacted regional water availability. Consequently, the different scientific models resulted in a "science impasse" with each side "convinced that their respective approach should guide water management decisions and policies".[133] The Review report did not go into detail regarding the scientific debate between Environment Canterbury and development interests, nor the negative impact it was having by stalling water allocation planning.[134]

The Review Group also identified the slow processing of resource consents.[135] First, the expansion of the dairy industry in the region increased the number of resource consent applications. Second, when Environment Canterbury notified the Natural Resources Regional Plan in 2004 it contained "sustainable take limits" which increased the number of water consent applications. Third, as water allocations reached sustainable limits in some areas the "first-come first-served" rule created a "gold rush" effect. For Environment Canterbury, the "first in, first served" priority rule led to applicants wanting to ensure they had access to water by applying for consents first:[136]

> This was exacerbated by the boom in dairy farming and other rural production (which required irrigated land), and the competing demands of energy generators, meant that water became a very valuable resource.

Environment Canterbury should have anticipated the land use changes to dairy conversion.[137] As a result of increased numbers of consent applications, consents were "bundled" but without using section 37A(2) of the RMA that allows for an extension of processing time where applicants agree. These problems with Canterbury water planning and consent processing resulted in direct central government intervention implementing the Environment Canterbury (Temporary Commissioners and Improved Water Management) Act 2010 to replace elected Council members with Commissioners to address freshwater management in the region.

Taranaki Regional Council Freshwater Plan and the "first in, first served" rule

The current Regional Freshwater Plan prepared by the Taranaki Regional Council implements the requirements of the National Policy Statement Freshwater Management 2014 through a Progressive Implementation Programme for a Draft Freshwater Land and Management Plan.[138] The Progressive Implementation Plan details the progress that has been made on planning for water allocation and water quality issues. Taranaki Regional Council has also prepared further plans that address aspects of the National Policy Statement Freshwater Management 2014. In 2017, the regional council released the Taranaki Regional Requirements for Good Farm Management, which addressed issues relating to dairy effluent, wetland protection and riparian management. It aims to fully implement the National Policy Statement Freshwater Management by the year 2025 or 2030.

The current Regional Freshwater Plan is extensive and includes the method and reasoning for adopting a particular policy approach. In Chapter 5, "The Use and Development of Freshwater", the contextual summary acknowledges the various industries relying upon water in the region including municipal water supply, hydroelectric power generation, water used in primary production industries such as freezing works, dairy and petroleum.[139] It does not specifically mention water takes for irrigation. The summary provides a detailed view of freshwater issues facing the region. However, there is no ranking of the most important. In comparison, some of the other regional plans lack a detailed context such as the one provided by Taranaki.[140] Policy 6.1.5(b) is unique in that it attempts to deal with competing demands for surface water as follows:

b) where there are competing uses for water, or in catchments identified in Policy 6.1.2, the degree of community or regional benefit from the taking, use, damming or diversion as distinct from private or individual benefit

The case law on competing claims to water clearly does not allow for a comparative assessment of competing applications.[141] However, in the Taranaki Council Regional Freshwater Plan, there is a specific rule allowing the consideration of competing use when processing an application for surface water takes.

The "Explanation" for Policy 6.1.5 is reproduced in full below because it is such a departure from rules in other regional plans, which generally do not focus on competing applications in such a direct manner. This section is also included because of the case law regarding competing applications and the emphasis on the priority rule for applications to be determined under the "first-come, first served" precedent.[142]

> Policy 6.1.5 sets out a number of specific matters which the Taranaki Regional Council will take into account in assessing resource consent applications for the taking, use, damming or diversion of water. These matters in the main relate to determining water allocation priorities among competing users and means whereby water users can avoid, remedy or mitigate any adverse environmental effects of the activity. The Taranaki Regional Council will consider the need to ensure that surface water is available for reasonable domestic needs, and for stock watering and firefighting purposes. Where there are competing uses for water, the Taranaki Regional Council will consider the degree of community or regional benefit from the activity as distinct from private benefits or benefits that arise primarily to individuals. Where there are no competing uses, the Taranaki Regional Council will allocate water on a "first-come, first-served" basis. In either event, water allocated may be transferred to other water users in accordance with Policy 6.1.9. Policy 6.1.5 requires further, that applicants justify the need for the water sought, ie, that the volumes sought are reasonable having regard to the intended use and local conditions, and that water be used efficiently with a minimum of waste. The Taranaki Regional Council will also take into account what alternative water supplies, or water collection or storage methods have been considered.

The policy statement above maintains that where there are no competing applications for water take the "first-come, first-served" rule applies. However, if the surface water body is approaching a situation where granting one application may exclude another, then wider community benefits can be taken into consideration.[143] However, the "first-come first-served" precedent does not distinguish between applications in the manner that the rule has on the basis of competing uses.[144] The "first-come, first-served" precedent requires regional councils to process applications in the order that they are received, without making comparisons with other potential applications. A rule allowing comparison of other applications conflicts with this decision-making process under the "first-come, first-served" precedent. From a legal perspective, such a conflict is problematic.

How does New Zealand determine priorities for water allocation and why is it important?

As explained above, regional plans and policy documents set the guidelines for when water can and cannot be taken. These rules specify when water allocations are allowed or require an application for a resource consent to be lodged with the regional council. Regional councils are not required to provide a list of priorities for water allocation. As a result of the lack of guidance on priority, the issue of priority between competing applications may be litigated in court. This section examines how the court determines issues of priority between competing applications. It shows that ultimately the court is not considering the merits of one application against another because the RMA does not allow for this type of comparison to occur. It also shows the development of precedent with its reliance on property-type concepts.

Fleetwing Farms v Marlborough District Council *and the* "*first-come, first-served*" *precedent*

Fleetwing Farms v Marlborough District Council was the first case under the RMA to consider the treatment of competing applications for the same resource.[145] In this case, the Marlborough District Council received two competing applications for mussel farming in the same area of seabed. Granting one application would exclude the other. Initially, Aqua King filed a resource consent application in September 1992 to establish a marine farm in Port Underwood. The Marlborough District Council requested further information from Aqua King before the application could be processed.[146] Then, in November 1992, Fleetwing Farms application for mussel farming, in the same area of Port Underwood, was also accepted by the Council.[147] Later, the Council advised Fleetwing Farms it made an error in accepting both applications for the same area of water. Eventually, both applications were heard and declined on the same day.

In the litigation history of this case, it proceeded on appeal to the Environment Court, High Court and Court of Appeal before being reconsidered by the Environment Court. The Court of Appeal directed the Environment Court to reconsider the applications to determine which applicant had priority under the relevant administrative provisions of the

RMA.[148] The Court of Appeal found that the statute provided timetabled requirements for resource consent processing and provided a careful analysis of relevant sections to show that a comparative analysis is not allowed under the RMA.[149] This assessment guided the Environment Court in determining which applicant had priority when the applications were for the same resource and similar activity.

The Environment Court considered the role of sustainable management in determining which applicant had priority:[150]

> The **purpose** of the Act is the promotion of sustainable management of natural resources – in this case the coastal marine area of Jerdens Bay. So what is required of a consent authority in processing applications for the allocation of natural resources is prompt advancement of, or active support for, the form of management set out in the timetabling provisions.

The Environment Court also considered whether the merits of one application should be compared to another potential applicant. The Court considered the previous law, the Marine Farming Act 1971, where the likelihood of financial success of an applicant's proposal was relevant in deciding whether or not to grant a resource consent.[151] However, the Environment Court found that the RMA did not contain a similar requirement to consider the financial success of an application. The Court concluded that there was "nothing in the Act to warrant refusing an application on the ground that another applicant would or might meet a higher standard than the Act specified".[152] Specifically, the RMA "does not regulate competing applications".[153] In the absence of a statutory rule for determining priority between competing uses for water allocation, priority by time emerged as the method by which priority between competing applications for a resource consent would be determined. Thus, the first applicant to have a complete application ready to be accepted for lodgement by the regional council should be the first to be heard, which is referred to as the "first-come, first-served" rule for water allocation. In subsequent cases, the Court has applied this precedent as parties focus on the administrative aspects of the RMA. The following decisions show the development of this priority rule for water allocation and its implications.

Aoraki Water Trust v Meridian Energy

An existing water permit allocating all the water in the catchment to Meridian Energy, a power generation company, was challenged by a later applicant wanting water for an irrigation scheme. The plaintiff, Aoraki

Water Trust, sought a declaration under section 311 of the RMA to provide certainty regarding the extent of rights granted under the water permit it held.

Aoraki argued that the nature of the rights held by Meridian Energy were "no more than a privilege and permission" subject to "natural events" and "any later grant of permits to others".[154] Aoraki argued there was a distinction between a "water right" and "water permit" and a "water permit" issued under the RMA was "not a property right".[155] In response, Meridian submitted that a water permit was a "legal determination" allocating all the water flowing through the catchment into Lake Tekapo.[156]

The Court decided against Aoraki. From a practical perspective, the Court found that accepting Aoraki's position, to reject the "first-come, first-served" priority rule, would place limits on the councils' ability to manage water allocation.[157] The Court's second line of reasoning examined the status of a water permit in property law. However, section 122(1) of the RMA expressly states that "A resource consent is neither real nor personal property". In applying property law concepts to a water permit, the Court determined that a further allocation of a water permit to Aoraki would derogate from the water permit held by Meridian Energy.[158] The Court applied the property law principle of "non-derogation" from a grant in determining Meridian Energy's position as the exclusive holder of water in Lake Tekapo, which confirmed their rights under their water permit. Lake Tekapo was fully allocated by the water permit held by Meridian Energy. The Court's decision confirmed the exclusive nature of Meridian Energy's access to the water allocated under the permit.

The decision was later critiqued by Barton for confusing property rights in a resource consent with the water itself and conflicting with the requirement under section 122 of the RMA.[159] There were sufficient administrative provisions that would have resulted in the same legal outcome without relying upon property rights.[160] It is important to understand that the non-derogation principle would not be followed in later cases, as discussed in *Hampton v Canterbury Regional Council* below. In *Aoraki Water Trust v Meridian Energy*, it is evident that the Courts were taking an approach which was not a part of the RMA water allocation framework. The evidence supporting the fact that there was a divergence from the RMA each time property law concepts were applied is the link with transferability. The inclusion of property-related concepts in allocation water would only have made sense from legal policy development if there was a concurrent development of transferability mechanisms for water permits.[161] Under the RMA, transferability of water permits has limited statutory recognition. Hence, it was always the administrative provisions of the RMA that underpinned water allocation, not property law-related concepts.

Southern Alps Air Ltd v Queenstown Lakes District Council

The principle of non-derogation was also considered in *Southern Alps Air Ltd v Queenstown Lakes District Council*.[162] Southern Alps Air Limited, a commercial jet boat operator, applied for a resource consent to operate on Lake Wanaka and the Wilkin River. The regional council declined the application. The Environment Court decision also denied Southern Alps Air the resource consent. The basis of the Environment Court decision was on two grounds, safety principles and non-derogation of the water permit.[163] The High Court reversed the Environment Court ruling on two grounds; the nature of rights in a resource consent and the application of maritime rules that could assist in addressing safety issues. In the High Court, River Jet argued that legal acceptance of the non-derogation argument "was not a question of law, but rather one of fact and degree".[164] The grant of a further consent would inhibit the river jet from being able to operate without any restrictions on the timing of activities. The High Court held there would be no significant derogation if a further resource consent were granted.[165] In reaching this decision, the Court considered *Dart River Safaris v Kemp* but distinguished it on its facts concluding that it had limited precedent value because it did not have a "derogation assessment".[166] However, the decision in *Aoraki Water Trust v Meridian Energy* was found to be relevant, and the High Court found that a derogation needs to be significant. The case was then referred back to the Environment Court to reconsider. The Environment Court declined Southern Alps Air's resource consent again on the basis that the aggregate effect on amenity values would be too high. The Environment Court also observed the following:[167]

> If the Queenstown Lakes District Council wishes to increase competition on the Wilkin River, the remedy is at least partly in its hands – for future applications on other rivers anyway. It should give single operators fewer trips and make them both for limited terms and non-aggregative.

From an initial application for a resource consent in 2005, the final decision of the Environment Court was received in 2010. The extensive litigation history also gave rise to significant costs to the parties. The principle of non-derogation was confirmed. This case advanced the non-derogation principle by clarifying that for derogation of a water permit to occur there must be a significant derogation.

Central Plains Water Trust v Ngai Tahu Properties

This case concerned competing applications for water from the Waimakariri and Rakaia Rivers. Central Plains Water Trust had applied to take water in 2001, which the Canterbury Regional Council later determined required notification. However, the Trust could not proceed with the notification until a further resource consent for the proposed water use was filed. In 2005, Ngai Tahu Properties filed a complete water take and use application to irrigate 5700 ha of land to convert forestry to pasture.[168] The Environment Court granted Ngai Tahu preliminary consent in a decision issued on 20 April 2006, which acknowledged that if Central Plains Water Trust had priority, then Ngai Tahu's conditions of consent would limit their access to water.[169] Ngai Tahu then filed for a declaration from the Environment Court that it had priority.[170] The key issue before the Courts was which application had priority based on being first to file or the first application ready for public notification. The Environment Court followed *Geotherm v Waikato Regional Council* in holding the notification stage was a trigger for determining priority between the parties. The Environment Court found that when Central Plains Water Trust's application was put on hold by the Canterbury Regional Council, it meant Ngai Tahu was first in reaching the notification stage and had priority over Central Plains Water Trust.[171]

The Environment Court granted the declaration confirming Ngai Tahu had priority. The subsequent appeal by Central Plains Water Trust in the Environment Court was unsuccessful. The High Court also found in favour of Ngai Tahi.[172] However, the issue of a larger development being trumped by a later less complex proposal continued to be of relevance. Leave to appeal to the Court of Appeal was granted with the acknowledgement that not only were matters of law requiring confirmation but also the scale of the proposed development meant many parties would be affected by the outcome of the decision.[173]

In the Court of Appeal, counsel for both sides accepted the "first-come, first-served" rule and presented arguments based on procedural issues.[174] While it was confirmed that "priority is on a first come, first served basis", the Court held that the priority rule by the earlier time of application is "subject to exception".[175] However, as neither party made submissions challenging the appropriateness of the "first-come, first-served" rule, this point was not addressed further by the Court. Consideration of larger developments was perceived as being in the public interest, which should not be "trumped or significantly interfered with by later small, simpler inconsistent proposals that can be made comprehensively without needing to proceed in stages".[176] Central Plains Water Trust was part of a larger irrigation development that would proceed in stages. Similar constraints did not bind the later applicant regarding the size and scale of their resource consent application. The Court of Appeal found in favour of Central Plains Water Trust reversing the decision of the lower courts because of factors relating to the scale of its proposal.

The legal implications of the "first-come, first-served" rule

The Court has expressed that it considers the "first-come, first-served" principle as a "working solution" to the legal problem of how to determine priority between competing water allocation applications:[177]

> [89] What has caused difficulty in this particular case is the application of that formula, which was evolved in a relatively simple context in *Fleetwing Farms Ltd v Marlborough District Council* [1997] 3 NZLR 257, to a vastly more complex context.

The "simple context" referred to in the quote above in *Fleetwing Farms v Marlborough District Council* was that both applicants were commercial competitors applying for a resource consent for essentially the same type of activity, marine farming. As both applicants were applying for similar purposes, it would not be correct to compare one application with another because the effects of granting a permit to either applicant would be the same or similar. However, in *Central Plains Water Trust v Ngai Tahu Properties*, the applicants were not taking water for the same use, and it is "arguable that *Fleetwing* does not deal with the situation where the applicants are not similar commercial competitors".[178]

The Supreme Court issued an interim judgment advising that the Court wished to hear arguments on whether the *Fleetwing Farms v Marlborough District Council* principle applied the grounds a consent authority should decide priority between competing applications.[179] However, before the decision was issued, the parties reached an agreement.

Hampton v Canterbury Regional Council

Simon Hampton (Simon) held a resource consent (granted in 2004) to take water to irrigate his land. An initial application made by Simon was amended to include his cousin's, Robert Hampton (Robert), neighbouring farm. In 2008, Simon applied for a portion of the resource consent to be transferred to a third party. Initial documents showed that Robert's land would no longer receive irrigation water.[180] However, later Robert was granted a servient consent that allowed him to take water when Simon was not irrigating his land. The consent granted to Robert meant that Simon was no longer able to transfer the water to the third party. Simon applied for a judicial review of the decision.

The High Court found that there was no guarantee that the consent would be transferred, and any transfer was still subject to meeting the requirements in the relevant regional plan.[181] The Court distinguished the facts of *Aoraki v Meridian Energy* on the basis that it was dealing with a situation where the resource was already fully allocated, and the grant of another consent would reduce the amount available to Meridian Energy.[182] The Court of Appeal confirmed the discretionary nature of regional council decision-making powers. Simon could not expect that the transfer would occur because "any right of transfer was clearly contingent on the grant of a consent to do so".[183] On the point of non-derogation, the Court addressed the decision in *Aoraki v Meridian Energy*, as discussed above, confirming that the decision was correct in the circumstances of a fully allocated catchment. The Court went on to astutely distinguish the facts of Simon's consent. In addressing the non-derogation argument, the Court focused first on the question of the nature of property rights in the resource consent by referring to section 122(1) of the RMA. The Court stated that a claim to property would only exist where the facts show that "contrary to s 122(1) of the Act, Simon's resource consent is seen as conferring a property right".[184] A further observation was that Simon had not agreed to charge Robert for the water linked to Robert's land.[185] It is relevant that Simon was unable to secure payment for the water that would be used by Robert. An alternative option for Simon was to enter into a contract with Robert, instead of a third party, to sell the water.

The Court of Appeal looked closely into the findings in *Aoraki Water Trust v Meridian Energy* focusing on the arguments around the concept of property and non-derogation. Meridian Energy argued their consents should be retained on the grounds of legitimate expectation. The application of legitimate expectation was declined by the Court of Appeal with regards to Simon's circumstances as explained above. *Hampton v Canterbury Regional Council* (Environment Canterbury) stated that the application of property law concepts and non-derogation to resource consents were "problematic" to rely upon.[186] The Court made several observations about the development of rights to water allocation. It confirmed that natural water could not be "owned as property" and recognised that section 21 of the Water and Soil Conservation Act 1967 vested the right to use natural water with the Crown. Finally, it traced the right of the Crown control of natural water in section 354(1)(b) of the RMA. The Court of Appeal goes further to identify that reasoning relating to the nature of property in a resource consent in *Aoraki v Meridian Energy* was incorrect:[187]

> In the circumstances, the statement made in *Aoraki* (drawing a parallel with profits à prendre) that a water permit allows the holder to remove "property", even though "owned by the Crown", is incorrect. For the same reason it was not correct to rely on the non-derogation principle

on the basis it was common to all relationships which confer a "right in property".

The Court of Appeal turned to statutory provisions, including section 122 of the RMA that declares there is neither real nor personal property under the Act except for circumstances where the Act provides these rights in limited circumstances.[188] The analysis of the Court showed that the Act provides for situations where a resource consent holder may exercise property-like rights, but these are limited to those situations where the statute defines the rights. An application for leave to appeal the decision in the Supreme Court by Simon was dismissed. The matter was not of "general importance", and the arguments raised against the *Aoraki* judgement "criticisms do not undermine the *Aoraki* decision itself".[189]

Is a water permit property?

The question of property in a resource consent has generated debate. The debate centres on the question of the interpretation of section 122 of the RMA. This section states that a resource consent is "neither real nor personal property". Fraser focused on the use of economic concepts to understand the apparent disconnect between a resource consent which has value to the holder and how the holder of that resource consent can protect his or her interests within the consent.[190] Barton's analysis of property rights in a resource consent focuses more closely on section 122 and its interpretation by the Court in order to show that property law-related concepts are not always appropriate when determining the nature of a resource consent.[191] These commentaries certainly illustrate the problems that affect water allocation in New Zealand. It has been suggested that *Hampton v Canterbury Regional Council* (Environment Canterbury) was a "missed opportunity to nudge informed debate about them".[192] The Court made several important observations about the public nature of rights in natural water. It also confirmed that the principle of "first-come, first-served" did apply to comparable applications with similar effects.

Other resource consent applications are defined by the purpose of the activity. The difference with water allocation, however, is that while the water take may be the same for competing applications, the use of that water take may be different. New Zealand has bundled water permits and this is a relevant factor in considering how to allocate water to competing applications. *Hampton v Canterbury Regional Council* (Environment Canterbury) clarified this point. The Court could not go beyond and look into the substantive reasoning for the ordering of priority because the statute does not allow it to do so. Just as Simon Hampton should have provided for a contract to charge Robert for the water applied to Robert's land, it is the role of regional councils to provide the substantive guidance on priority for water allocation.

Summary

At the top of the tiered hierarchy of plans contained within the RMA, it was national policy that would have provided guidance for regional councils. However, the national policy for water management was not promulgated until 2011. This led to a significant policy gap at the highest level from 1991 until 2011. The inability to provide national guidance has significantly hampered the setting of priorities for water allocation in New Zealand. In light of the policy gap, the administrative provisions within the RMA gained greater importance in guiding regional council decision making. The interpretation of these administrative provisions in the case of *Fleetwing Farms v Marlborough District Council* established the "first in, first served" precedent. The precedent is problematic in situations where regional water allocation is close to full allocation or over-allocated. It is challenged on the basis of being a method of water allocation that is inherently unsustainable because it does not allow regional councils to consider alternative uses for water. It also does not allow regional councils to compare one application to another. As a result, it is highly questionable whether New Zealand has achieved a method of sustainable or good water allocation because potential future use and demand for water cannot be taken into account in regional council decision making.

Notes

1 For the purpose of this book, the RMA does not have a water allocation frame-work stated in the traditional sense. The reference to the framework encapsu-lates the collective water policies and plans that were meant to be prepared following the provisions within the RMA. It has been described as both a "framework" and an "umbrella" statute. See Ceri Warnock and Maree Galloway *Focus on Resource Management Law* (LexisNexis, Wellington, 2015) at 145.

2 Resource Management Act 1991, Part 4 of the Act states the "Functions, pow-ers and duties of central and local government".

3 David Grinlinton "Legitimate planning guidance or potential constitutional vandalism? National Policy Statements after *King Salmon*" (2015) 11 BRMB 83 at 83.

4 National Policy Statement for Freshwater Management 2011. Revised in 2014 and reviewed in 2017.

5 Establishing regional plans is one of the "functions" of regional councils under section 30 of the RMA. A key distinction in the New Zealand context is that a "function" does not confer a legal obligation to create the regional plan. District plans must have regard to regional policy and not be inconsistent with National

Policy Statements. See Resource Management Act section 73(4). Christina Robb *Water Allocation a Strategic Overview* (Ministry for the Environment, Wellington, 2001) at 12 states the weakness of regional plans as follows: Regional plans did not exist in all regions, if a regional plan was prepared they "varied considerably in their form and scope", that the values and objectives in regional plans are "unclear", that there was a lack of "linkages between objectives, policies and methods", monitoring issues were "often not addressed" and that the regional plans focus more on the regulatory aspects of resource consent decision making.

6   Robb, above at 12.

7   *Fleetwing Farms Ltd v Marlborough District Council* [1997] 3 NZLR 257 (CA). The development of the "first in, first served" precedent is provided later in this chapter.

8   Robb, above n 5, at 9.

9   National Policy Statement for Freshwater Management 2011. Revised in 2014 and reviewed in 2017.

10 *Fleetwing Farms Ltd v Marlborough District Council* [1997] 3 NZLR 257 (CA).

11 Ministry for the Environment *Water Programme of Action. Water Allocation and Use Technical Working Paper June 2004* (Ministry for the Environment, Wellington, 2004) at 6.

12 Brisbane Declaration "The Brisbane Declaration: Environmental Flows Are Essential for Freshwater Ecosystem Health and Human Well-Being" (2007) *Declaration of the 10th International River Symposium and International Environmental Flows Conference*, 3–6 September 2007, Brisbane, Australia defined "Environmental Flows" as "the quantity, timing, and quality of water flows required to sustain freshwater and estuarine ecosystems and the human livelihoods and well-being that depend on these ecosystems".

13 In Ministry for the Environment, *Proposed National Environmental Standard on Ecological Flows and Water Levels* (Ministry for the Environment, Wellington, 2008) at 7, the term "environmental flow" is used as an alternative to "minimum flow" to recognise the range of "values" that contribute to setting of environmental flows.

14 See Ministry for the Environment, above for the effect on surface water allocation. For the specific effect on groundwater abstraction and the monitoring of bores see A.D. Fenemor and C.A. Robb "Groundwater Management in New Zealand" in M.R. Rosen and P.A. White (eds) *Groundwaters of New Zealand* (New Zealand Hydrological Society Inc., Wellington, 2001) 273 at 279.

15 Ministry for the Environment and Ministry of Agriculture and Fisheries *Wai Ora: Report of the Sustainable Water Programme of Action Consultation Hui* (Ministry for the Environment, Wellington, 2005). Ministry for the Environment "Sustainable Water Program of Action – An Implementation Package" (n.d.) www.mfe.govt.nz/more/cabinet-papers-and-related-material-search/cabine t-papers/freshwater/sustainable-water-0 discussed the need to address the growing demand for water; Cabinet Paper "Regulatory impact statement for draft National Environmental Standard on Measuring Water Takes" (February 2008) CAB POL (08).

16 Lincoln Environmental *Information on Water Allocation in New Zealand Report No 4375/1* (Ministry for the Environment, Wellington, 2000) at 35.

17 Ministry for the Environment above n 15 at 15–17 identified the problems with environmental flow setting as "3.1.1 Resource consent decisions are being

made on water bodies for which there is no environmental flow or water level in place"; "3.1.2 Existing environmental flows and water levels do not always clearly define the available water" and "3.1.3 Existing process for setting ecological flows for water levels is costly and contentious".

18 Rick M. Fisher and Shona Russell "Water Policy and Regulatory Reform in New Zealand" (2011) 27(2) *Int. J Water Res.* 387 at 388; and Andrew Hayward "Freshwater Management: water Markets and Novel Pricing Regimes" (2006) 10 *NZJEL* 215 at 220 describes the outcome of the SWOPA as providing only "vague" proposals.

19 Gary Taylor "Environmental Policy-Making in New Zealand, 1978–2013" (2013) 9(3) *Policy Quarterly* 18 at 21.

20 The implementation of national policy was outlined in Ministry for the Environment, Minister of Agriculture *Sustainable Water Program of Action – Implementation Package* above n 15.

21 Instead, the setting of environmental flows was transferred to "A New Start for Freshwater" policy programme introduced in 2008. See Cabinet Paper "Implementing the New Start for Fresh Water: proposed Official's Work Plan" (n.d.).

22 Ministry for the Environment "Environmental Stewardship for a Prosperous New Zealand. Briefing for Incoming Minister for the Environment November 2008" (Ministry for the Environment, Wellington, 2008) stated that freshwater demand was increasing and further attention was needed to address water quality and allocation issues.

23 Taylor, above n 19. This agreement was reached at the 2008 Environmental Defence Society Conference.

24 Cabinet Paper, above n 28. National won the 2008 general election, which ended nine years of Labour-led government in New Zealand.

25 Cabinet Paper *New Start for Fresh Water Cabinet Paper* (2010).

26 A.D. Fenemor, T. Davie and S. Markham "Hydrological Information in Water Law and Policy: new Zealand's Devolved Approach to Water Management" in J. Wallace and P. Wouters (eds) *Hydrology and Water Law: Bridging the Gap* (IWA Publishing, London, 2006).

27 Resource Management (Measurement and Reporting of Water Takes) Regulations 2010, section 4 states that takes above 5 cubic metres per second should be recorded and reported to the regional council. Under section 6, water permit holders must keep records of water taken on a daily or weekly basis that can be consolidated into an annual amount.

28 Erwin Corong, Mike Henson and Phil Journeaux *Value of Irrigation to New Zealand. Economy-wide Assessment* (NZIER, AgFirst, Wellington, 2014) at 3.

29 New Zealand Herald "Large-scale water theft in Canterbury – but no prosecutions" *New Zealand Herald* (20 June 2016); Charlie Mitchell "Over the line: rivers being whittled away" www.stuff.co.nz (6 February 2017).

30 Charlie Mitchell "Millions of litres of water illegally taken: is Ecan doing enough"? *NZ Farmer* (20 June 2016).

31 Ministry for the Environment & Statistics NZ (2017) *New Zealand's Environmental Reporting Series: our fresh water 2017.* (Ministry for the Environment, Statistics New Zealand, Wellington, 2017). Prior to 2017, both the Ministry and the Statistics Department published separate reports. The Environmental Reporting Act 2015 section 10(1)(c) requires the joint publication of a report in specific areas including "the freshwater domain".

32 At 59.
33 OECD, above at 2.
34 OECD *Environmental Performance Review* (OECD Publishing, Paris, 2017) at 3. Media Release: EDS commends OECD Environmental Performance Review of New Zealand (21 March 2017) states The Director of the OECD Environment Directorate at the time the Report was published was Hon Simon Upton. He was "one of the architects of the Resource Management Act (along with Sir Geoffrey Palmer)". Later, Simon Upton was sworn in as New Zealand's Parliamentary Commissioner for the Environment on 16 October 2017. Parliamentary Commissioner for the Environment "About us. The Commissioner".
35 Above.
36 Above at 195.
37 Above at 195.
38 I.H. Williams "The Resource Management Act 1991: well Meant but Hardly Done" (2000) 9 (4) *The Otago L. Rev.* 673 at 674.
39 Geoffrey Palmer, QC "The Resource Legislation Amendment Bill, the Productivity Commission Report and the Future of Planning for the Environment in New Zealand" (2018) 12(4) *Policy Quarterly* 71 at 72. Refers to the "failure" of the RMA in terms of the failure of central government and regional government to "make policy statements, set environmental standards that the Act provides for". Without the policy statements at both levels, the inference is that the RMA resource allocation framework is incomplete. This is particularly a problem for water allocation planning as discussed in this chapter with policy gaps at both the central government and some regional government levels.
40 Robb, above n 5, at 6.
41 Devolution of power was to address the pre-existing problems with "ad hoc" government intervention in environmental planning. Hon Simon Upton stated the problems with environmental law prior to the RMA as a "plethora of rules" with "conflicting objectives". (4 July 1991) 516 NZPD 3018, Hon Simon Upton.
42 Resource Management Act 1991, section 42C states the functions of the Environmental Protection Agency. The current EPA was established by the Environmental Protection Authority Act 2011, which replaced the EPA established under the RMA. The EPA decision on the Tukituku Catchment is discussed later in this chapter.
43 Resource Management Act 1991 section 42C(c).
44 Resource Management Act 1991, Part 11.
45 Resource Management Act 1991, Part 5, Subpart I "National direction".
46 For example, the Resource Management Amendment Act 2005 was directly relevant to water allocation as it amended section 30 to add section 30(1)(fa) to amend the function of regional councils to make rules to allocate water.
47 Ministry for the Environment *Resource Legislation Amendments 2017 – Factsheet 1* (Ministry for the Environment, Wellington, 2017) at 9.
48 Above at 9.
49 Resource Management Act 1991, section 46A(3).
50 Section 46A(4)(a)(ii).
51 Section 47(1).
52 Section 47(2)(a).

53 Section 47A.

54 Section 48.

55 Section 51 outlines matters to be considered in the report.

56 Sections 58B–58J.

57 Geoffrey Palmer *Protecting New Zealand's Environment. An Analysis of the Government's Proposed Freshwater Management and Resource Management Act 1991 Reforms* (New Zealand Fish and Game Council, Wellington, 2013) at 24 states the 2005 Amendments "expanded the function of the Minister for the Environment creating a new power for the Minister to direct plan changes", which was "universally opposed by all sectors".

58 Andrea P. Sumits and Jason I. Morrison *Creating a Framework for Sustainability in California: lessons Learned from the New Zealand Experience. A Report of the Pacific Institute for Studies in Development, Environment and Security* (Pacific Institute, California, 2001) at v.

59 Above.

60 Palmer, above n 57 at 72: He goes on to observe "Political reactions that have led to numerous amending acts for the RMA over the years have made the legislation worse, not better. Constant fiddling debilitates both the act and administration".

61 Resource Management Act 1991, section 30, 63.

62 Robb, above n 5, at 12.

63 Resource Management Act 1991, section 65 states that "A regional council may prepare a regional plan for the whole or part of its region for any function specified in section 30(1)(c), (ca), (e), (f), (fa), (fb), (g), or (ga)".

64 These changes were contained in section 30(1)(fa) and section 30(4) of the RMA. The Amendment began as a bill focusing on energy and resources. It was formerly a part of the Resource Management and Electricity Legislation Amendment Bill 2005. Later, the Bill was split into two; the Resource Management Amendment Bill (No. 5) and the Electricity Amendment Bill (No. 3).

65 Regional councils may classify a particular activity such as the taking of a set volume of water as a permitted, controlled, restricted discretionary, discretionary, non-complying or prohibited activity under the Resource Management Act 1991, section 77A.

66 T.H. Snelder, H.L. Rouse, P.A. Franklin, D.J. Booker, N. Norton and J. Diettrich. "The role of science in setting water resource use limits: case studies from New Zealand" (2014) 59 (3.4) Hydrological Sciences Journal 844 at 885 states these limits set "regulatory criteria that determine how water resources are allocated to environmental flow and out-of-channel use".

67 Ministry for the Environment *Discussion Document on the Proposed National Environmental Standard on Ecological Flows and Water Levels* (Ministry for the Environment, Wellington, 2006).

68 Sinclair Knight Merz "Alternatives to the 'first in, first served' approach to water allocation" *Options to Improve Water Allocation Outcomes* (Ministry for the Environment, Ministry for Economic Development and Ministry of Agriculture and Fisheries, Wellington, 2005) at 3.

69 Above at 3.

70 Resource Management (Waitaki Catchment) Amendment Act 2004, section 3, section 8; Resource Management Waitaki Catchment Amendment Bill 2004 (Select Committee Report 2002–2005 Vol XIV) at 1011 states "There is

currently no regional plan for the allocation of water in the Waitaki Catchment, nor is there a minimum flow regime for the river".

71 Above at 1012. Resource Management Waitaki Catchment Amendment Bill 2004 (Select Committee Report 2002–2005 Vol XIV) at 1023. The Opposition Party strongly objected to the Bill on the following grounds that rules were being rewritten for a "huge state owned enterprise project" leading to "skewed" decision making in the issuing of resource consents. Claire Kilner "The RMA Under Review: A Case Study of Project Aqua" (2006) 58(2) Political Science 29 states one of the pressing regional issues that needed attention was a proposal to build a new dam, Project Aqua, which was later abandoned due to concerns over access to water rights and rising costs.

72 Christine Cheyne "Changing Urban Governance in New Zealand: Public Participation and Democratic Legitimacy in Local Authority Planning and Decision Making 1989–2014" (2015) 33(4) *Urban Policy and Research* 416 at 426.

73 Sinclair Knight Merz, above n 68, at 3.

74 Above at 3.

75 Above at 3.

76 Above at 3.

77 For best practice guide on preparing a section 32 analysis see Ministry for the Environment A guide to section 32 of the Resource Management Act 1991. Incorporating changes as a result of the Resource Legislation Amendment Act 2017 (Ministry for the Environment, Wellington, 2017). Ann Winstanley, Annabel Ahuriri-Driscoll, Maria Hepi, Virginia Baker and Jeffrey Foote. "Understanding the impact of democratic logics on participatory resource decision-making in New Zealand". (2016) 21(10) *Local Environment* 1171.

78 Resource Management Act 1991, section 32(1).

79 Ross Wilson Cost Benefit Approaches to Valuing Nature: Case Studies in New Zealand (Auckland Council, Auckland, 2012) at 5.

80 Resource Management Act 1991, section 32(2).

81 Quality Planning "Quality Planning Website Note on Section 32 Analysis" www.qualityplanning.org.nz/index.php/35-plan-development/74-guidanceno te-onsec32

82 Resource Management Act 1991, section 32(2).

83 Klaus Bosselman "Sustainability Alternatives: A German-New Zealand Perspective" (2015) 13 New Zealand Journal of Public and International Law 25 at 32.

84 Resource Management Act 1991, section 14; Laws of New Zealand *Water* (online ed). These provisions are considered to be similar to rights to take water for domestic use that existed under the Water and Soil Conservation Act 1967.

85 Section 14(3)(a) allows the taking of water that has been "expressly allowed by a resource consent".

86 Statutory rights to suspend water takes during a shortage were carried through from the Water and Soil Conservation Act 1967 into the RMA under section 329. The Water and Soil Conservation Act 1967, section 23E gave specific powers to water boards to suspend water takes, "if, in the opinion of the Board, there is at any time a serious temporary shortage of water".

87 Barry Barton "Property Rights Created Under Statute in Common Law Legal Systems" in Aileen McHarg, Barry Barton, Adrian Bradbrook and Lee Godden

Property and the Law in Energy and Natural Resources (Oxford University Press, Oxford, 2010).

88 Resource Management Act 1991, section 136(2).

89 Waikato Regional Council *Waikato Regional Council Variation 6* (Waikato Regional Council, Hamilton, 2012). Policy 3.4.3 Transfer of Water Permits. Water transfers can assist with achieving the efficient use of water. Environment Southland Regional Council Proposed Southland Water and Land Plan (Environment Southland Regional Council, Invercargill, 2016). Policy 43 allows transfers subject to minimum flow and allocation rules.

90 Bay of Plenty Regional Council *Region-wide Water Quantity – Proposed Plan Change 9 Version 3.8* (Bay of Plenty Regional Council, Tauranga, 2017). Policy WQ P13 states enabling transfers as a means to improve efficiency. WQ P23(e) requires a "portion of the allocated water to be surrendered" in over-allocated catchments.

91 Greater Wellington Regional Council *Proposed Natural Resources Plan for the Wellington Region 31 July 2015* (Greater Wellington Regional Council, Wellington, 2015). Policy P128 encourages the transfer of water permits in the same catchment management unit so long as the transfer is reasonable and meets efficient use criteria in Schedule Q of the Plan.

92 *The Favourite Ltd v Vavasour* [2005] NZRMA 461.

93 At [30].

94 *Altimarloch Joint Venture Ltd v Moorhouse* HC Blenheim CIV-2005-406-91, 3 July 2008.

95 *Altimarloch Joint Venture Ltd v Moorhouse* HC Blenheim CIV-2005-406-91, 23 March 2009 [recall judgment]. The vendors were also sued for misrepresentation under section 6(1) of the Contractual Remedies Act 1979. During the conveyancing process, the vendors were not shown the water permit documents which had been signed on their behalf. It was not until after settlement that the discrepancy regarding the extent of water rights emerged.

96 *Vining Realty Group Ltd v Moorhouse* [2010] NZCA 104.

97 *Marlborough District Council v Vining Realty Group* [2012] NZSC 11. The RMA does not include provisions in relation to royalties or the pricing of water. In comparison, other resources such as geothermal do have provisions that allow regional councils to charge a royalty but these are not currently put into effect. Hence, in practice there is also no royalty on geothermal allocations either. See Katherine Luketina and Phoebe Parson "New Zealand's Public Participation in Geothermal Resource Development" in Adele Manzella, Agnes Allansdottir and Anna Pellizzone (eds) *Geothermal Energy and Society* (Springer, Italy, 2019) at 211.

98 The National Water and Soil Conservation Authority had the power to set permitted flow levels under the Water and Soil Conservation Act 1967, section 14(3)(o).

99 Water and Soil Conservation Act 1967, section 14(3)(a).

100 *Electricity Corporation of New Zealand Ltd v Manawatu-Wanganui Regional Council* W70/90 NZPT at 4.

101 At 22.

102 At 22. "The Act does not state the criteria by which the minimum acceptable flows of rivers and streams are fixed".

103 At 68.

104 At 81.

105 See *Otago Water Resource Users Group v Otago Regional Council* C88/2003, (4 July 2003) C21/2002 on mining privileges; *Minister of Conservation v Otago Regional Council* C71/2002, (25 June 2002) on minimum flows and *Fish and Game New Zealand (Central South Island Region) v Otago Regional Council* C79/2002, EnvC, (28 June 2002), the Kakanui Flows case will be discussed further below.

106 *Minister of Conservation v Otago Regional Council* C71/2002, (25 June 2002) at [19].

107 Otago Regional Council *Regional Plan: Water for Otago* (Otago Regional Council, Otago, 2004). There have been 14 plan changes since the plan became operative in 2004. A list of the plan changes is available at Otago Regional Council "Regional Plan: Water" https://www.orc.govt.nz/plans-policies-report s/regional-plans/water

108 At iii.

109 *Carter Holt Harvey v Waikato Regional Council* [2011] EnvC 380.

110 For further information on the Act and the settlement process see Linda Te Aho "Indigenous Challenges to Enhance Freshwater Governance and Management in Aotearoa New Zealand – The Waikato River Settlement" (2010) *The Journal of Water Law* 20; Jacinta Ruru "Indigenous restitution in settling water claims: the developing cultural and commercial redress opportunities in Aotearoa, New Zealand" (2013) 22 *Pacific Rim Law and Policy Journal* 311.

111 In Australian water law, major water takes are referred to as "bulk water" takes.

112 Sinclair Knight Merz "Alternatives to the 'first in, first served' approach to water allocation" *Options to Improve Water Allocation Outcomes* (Ministry for the Environment, Ministry for Economic Development and Ministry of Agriculture and Fisheries, Wellington, 2005).

113 The Canterbury region is discussed below as an example of a region where water allocation plans were not prepared. The Bay of Plenty Regional Council *Region-wide Water Quantity – Proposed Plan Change 9 Version 3.8* (Bay of Plenty Regional Council, Tauranga, 2017) is under appeal from a number of parties including the Tauranga City Council. The Council is concerned about the potential effect of the proposed Plan affecting the ability for the Council to provide water for urban use into the future. It is arguing that the Proposed Plan is inconsistent with obligations as a future urban growth area under the National Policy Statement for Urban Development Capacity 2016. There are also concerns over the inconsistencies with Council obligations to provide safe drinking water under the Health Act 1956 and the Local Government Act 2002. See *Tauranga City Council v Bay of Plenty Regional Council* Notice of Appeal on behalf of Tauranga City Council Against Decision on Proposed Plan Change 9 (Region-Wide Water Quantity) (15 November 2018).

114 Cabinet Paper "Improving the Resource Management Act 1991" (CAB Min (04) 30/10) at [26]. Cabinet Papers also stated that there was "uncertainty over water allocation issues in the absence of regional plans" in some areas. Examples discussed in this chapter include the Waitaki and Canterbury regions.

115 Ministry for the Environment & Statistics NZ (2017) *New Zealand's Environmental Reporting Series: Our Fresh Water 2017*.(Ministry for the Environment, Statistics New Zealand, Wellington, 2017) at 61 states the greatest "consented" use of water is from irrigation and hydro-electricity.

116 Manawatu-Whanganui Regional Council *One Plan 2014* (Horizons Regional Council, Palmerstone North, 2014) at 5-2.

117 Bay of Plenty Regional Council *Region-wide Water Quantity – Proposed Plan Change 9 Version 3.8* (Bay of Plenty Regional Council, Tauranga, 2017). Water Quality Rule 1 defines reasonable domestic needs as a restriction on property size to 5 hectares and the take is not more than 15 cubic metres per day. Environment Southland Regional Council Proposed Southland Water and Land Plan (Environment Southland Regional Council, Invercargill, 2016) sets the restrictions on surface water takes at not more than 2000 litres daily and 250 litres per hectare daily, up to a total limit of 40 cubic metres daily per "landholding" under Rule 49(a)(i). Greater Wellington Regional Council *Proposed Natural Resources Plan for the Wellington Region 31 July 2015* (Greater Wellington Regional Council, Wellington, 2015) at Rule 136. For example, for a property greater than 20 hectares, the limit on the volume per day is 20 cubic metres. On the other hand, properties less than 20 hectares have a daily limit of 10 cubic metres. The current Canterbury Land and Water Regional Plan allows "small and community water takes" for surface water at specified volumes according to the flow of the waterbody in Rule 5.111. Groundwater takes are permitted if the take is less than 100 cubic metres daily if the property is more than 20 hectares and the bore is less than 20 metres away from the property boundary under Rule 5.113. The Hawkes Bay Regional Management Plan republished in 2015 includes amendments for the Tukituki catchment. The take and use rules in the Plan in Rule 6.7.1 allows for domestic water take not exceeding 20 cubic metres daily per property.

118 Regional plans that have separate rules for dairyshed washdown water include the Waikato Regional Council Regional Plan Variation 6 and the Bay of Plenty Regional Council Proposed Plan Change 9.

119 Dominic Harris "Ecan accused of 'bending the law' over consents for water bottling plants" *stuff.co.nz* (16 March 2018) and Patrick Gower "Government 'not concerned' over massive water consent sale" *Newshub* (15 March 2017).

120 Ministry for the Environment & Statistics NZ (2017) *New Zealand's Environmental Reporting Series: Our Fresh Water 2017*, above n 36, at 59 stated "More than half the water allocated (or consented) by councils is for irrigation, but we do not know how much of this is actually used".

121 Auditor General *Monitoring How Water Is Used for Irrigation* (Auditor General, Wellington, 2018). It confirmed that water metres had largely been installed in the six regional councils they audited. The collection and use of data was the next step in improving the outcomes for water management based on that data.

122 Manawatu-Whanagnui Regional Council *One Plan 2014* (Horizons Regional Council, Palmerston North, 2014) at 5-2; Decision of the Environment Court Manawatu-Wanganui Proposed One Plan Appeals, Part 5 Surface Water Quality – Non Point Source Discharges; *Andrew Day v Manawatu-Wanganui District Council* 31 August 2012 [2012] EnvC 182.

123 *Horticulture New Zealand v Manawatu-Wangani Regional Council* [2013] NZHC 2942 [24 September 2013] at [20].

124 *Wellington Fish and Game Council v Manawatu Wanganui Regional Council* [2017] NZEnvC 37. Wellington Fish and Game Council sought a declaration under section 310 of the RMA for the Court to investigate if a "power or function" under the Act was omitted or contravened.

125 Minister for the Environment, Minister of Agriculture Appendix 1 Background on Sustainable Water Program of Action in New Start for Freshwater Cabinet Paper (n.d.).

These problems were "contrary" to the expectations of central government. See Ministry for the Environment *Briefing Paper: Joint Ministers meeting with MAF and MfE Reference 08-B-0260* (Ministry for the Environment, Wellington, 2008).

126 Cameron Holly and Andrew Lawson. "Implementing environmental law and collaborative governance" (2015) Implementing Environmental Law 238. For example, the Canterbury Water Management Strategy was an example of collaborative governance developed with the guidance of the Canterbury Mayoral Forum and published in November 2009.

127 Ann Brower "Is collaboration good for the environment? Or, what's wrong with the Land and Water Forum?" (2016) 40(3) NZJE 390.

128 Rt. Hon Wyatt Creech (Chair), Doug Martin, Greg Hill and Doug Low. *Investigation of the Performance of Environment Canterbury under the Resource Management Act and Local Government Act* (prepared for Ministry for the Environment, Wellington, 2010). At [6].

129 Above.

130 Edward P. Weber, Ali Memon and Brett Painter "Science, Society, and Water Resources in New Zealand: Recognizing and Overcoming A Societal Impasse" (2011) 13 *J. Environ. Pol. Plann.* 49-6. Quotes used in this paragraph are at 50.

131 At 50.

132 At 50.

133 At 50.

134 At 36: Policy and Plan Development is described as narrow and conservative. The quality of resource consent processing was affected by a wider "culture" including perception that "the organisation (resource consenting) is science led rather than science informed".

135 At 27.

136 At 27.

137 At 27.

138 First released in 2015 as the Taranaki Regional Council *Implementation Programme for the National Policy Statement Freshwater Management* (Taranaki Regional Council, New Plymouth, 2015). The Implementation Program was revised in 2018 in response to the review of the National Policy Statement Freshwater Management 2014.Taranaki Regional Council *Progressive Implementation Programme for the National Policy Statement Freshwater Management* (Taranaki Regional Council, New Plymouth, 2018).

139 Taranaki Regional Council *Regional Freshwater Plan* (Taranaki Regional Council, New Plymouth, 2001) at 37.

140 For example, the Northland Regional Council decided not to take this approach as indicated in the introduction to its regional plan. In terms of specific water allocation issues, the Water Resources Plan states the "potential for conflict between competing users" at times when there are lower flow levels.

141 See discussion in next section at 8.0 "How does New Zealand determine priorities for freshwater allocation and why is it important?"

142 For a full account of the "first-come, first-served" precedent see discussion in the next section of this chapter on "How does New Zealand determine priorities for water allocation and why is it important?"

143 The taking and use of groundwater is addressed separately in the Water Resources Plan. Groundwater availability is under less stress than surface water. The take and use of groundwater is regulated to ensure that its take

and use remains within the sustainable extraction limit for the aquifer. Rule 46 of the Plan permits the take of water of up to 50 cubic metres per day. The Taranaki Regional Council has not included the competing water takes rule (used for surface water allocation) in the groundwater allocation rules.

144 See discussion below at 8.0 of this chapter "How does New Zealand determine priorities for water allocation and why is it important?"

145 *Fleetwing Farms Ltd v Marlborough District Council* [1997] 3 NZLR 257 (CA).

146 *Fleetwing Farms Ltd v Marlborough District Council* W101/97 [1997] EnvC 362 (26 November 1997) at 3.

147 *Fleetwing Farms Ltd v Marlborough District Council* [1996] NZRMA 369 (HC).

148 *Fleetwing Farms Limited v Marlborough District Council* W101/97 [1997] EnvC 362 (26 November 1997) at 3.The decision as to priority between Fleetwing Farms and Aqua King was referred back to the Environment Court following the Court of Appeal decision in *Fleetwing Farms Ltd v Marlborough District Council* [1997] 3 NZLR 257 (CA).

149 *Fleetwing Farms Ltd v Marlborough District Council* [1997] 3 NZLR 257 (CA).

150 *Fleetwing Farms Limited v Marlborough District Council* W101/97 [1997] EnvC 362 (26 November 1997) at 8.

151 Marine Farming Act 1971, s 8(3).

152 At 8.

153 *Fleetwing Farms Limited v Marlborough District Council* W101/97 [1997] EnvC 362 (26 November 1997) at 8. See also *Geotherm Group Ltd v Waikato Regional Council* (2002) 9 ELRNZ 75 (EnvC) which confirmed priority should be given to the application first in time that is ready for notification.

154 At [22].

155 At [22].

156 At [23].

157 At [28].

158 At [34].

159 Barry Bartton "The Nature of Resource Consents: Statutory Permits or Property Rights" paper presented to New Zealand Law Society Environmental Law: National Issues Intensive Conference, July 2001, 51.

160 Barry Barton "Different kinds of argument for applying property law to resource consents" (2016) RMJ 1 at 1.

161 Above at 2.

162 *Southern Alps Air Ltd v Queenstown Lakes District Council* (2007) 13 ELRNZ 221; [2008] NZRMA 47 (HC).

163 *Southern Alps Air Ltd v Queenstown Lakes District Council* [2007] NZRMA 119 (EnvC).

164 *Southern Alps Air Ltd v Queenstown Lakes District Council* (2007) 13 ELRNZ 221: [2008] NZRMA 47 (HC) at [33].

165 At [47].

166 *Dart River Safaris v Kemp & Anor* [2000] NZRMA 440 (HC). *Southern Alps Air Ltd v Queenstown Lakes District Council* (2007) 13 ELRNZ 221c[2008]: NZRMA 47 (HC) at [37].

167 *Southern Alps Air Ltd v Queenstown Lakes District Council* [2010] EnvC 381: ENV-2006-CHC-7, 8 November 2010 at [102].

168 *Re Ngai Tahu Property Ltd Christchurch* C104/06, (EnvC) (21 August 2006) at [2].

169 At [6].

170 Above.

171 At [80].

172 *Central Plains Water Trust v Ngai Tahu Properties Ltd* (2006) 13 ELRNZ 63 (HC).

173 *Central Plains Water Trust v Ngai Tahu Properties Ltd* Christchurch CIV-2006-409-2116, 8 February 2007 (HC).

174 *Central Plains Water Trust v Ngai Tahu Properties Ltd* [2008] NZCA 71; (2008) 14 ELRNZ 61; [2008] NZRMA 200 at [7].

175 At [26] and [27] per Baragwanath J.

176 At [59].

177 *Central Plains Water Trust v Ngai Tahu Properties Ltd* [2008] NZCA 71; (2008) 14 ELRNZ 61; [2008] NZRMA 200 at [89].

178 At [37].

179 *Ngai Tahu Property Ltd v Central Plains Water Trust* [2008] NZSC 24. An amicus curiae was also to be appointed in order to address these issues.

180 *Hampton v Canterbury Regional Council* (Environment Canterbury) [2013] NZRMA 482 (HC) at [13].

181 At [71].

182 At [80].

183 *Hampton v Canterbury Regional Council* (Environment Canterbury) [2015] NZCA 509; (2015) 18 ELRNZ 825; [2016] NZRMA 369 at [86].

184 *Hampton v Canterbury Regional Council* (Environment Canterbury) [2015] NZCA 509; (2015) 18 ELRNZ 825; [2016] NZRMA 369 at [89].

185 At [89].

186 *Hampton v Canterbury Regional Council* (Environment Canterbury) [2015] NZCA 509; (2015) 18 ELRNZ 825; [2016] NZRMA 369 at [99]–[103].

187 *Hampton v Canterbury Regional Council* (Environment Canterbury) [2015] NZCA 509; (2015) 18 ELRNZ 825; [2016] NZRMA 369 at [103] Citing *Aoraki Water Trust v Meridian Energy* [2005] 2 NZLR 268 (HC) at [35]–[36].

188 *Hampton v Canterbury Regional Council* (Environment Canterbury) [2015] NZCA 509; (2015) 18 ELRNZ 825; [2016] NZRMA 369 at [105].

189 *Simon Hampton v Canterbury Regional Council* [2016] NZSC 50 at [7].

190 Laura Fraser "Property Rights in Environmental Management: The Nature of Resource Consents in the Resource Management Act 1991" (2008) NZJEL 12.

191 Barry Barton "The Nature of Resource Consents: Statutory Permits or Property Rights" (paper presented to New Zealand Law Society Environmental Law: National Issues Intensive Conference, July 2009) 51.

192 Trevor Daya-Winterbottom "New Zealand-freshwater allocation: Property rights, non-derogation from grant and legitimate expectation" (2015) 25(1) *Journal of Water Law* 38 at 40.

3 New Zealand water allocation law and policy after 2011

Introduction

This chapter focuses on the government response to water allocation problems identified in the previous chapter. The overarching problem was the consequences of the water allocation policy gap at the national and regional level from 1991 to 2011.[1] During the period of the policy gap, "limited guidance" on water allocation policy came from central government putting regional councils under pressure to make "almost all the most technically and politically difficult decisions on water management".[2] The previous chapter showed that the policy gap, together with water allocation under a "first come, first served" method, contributed to further over-allocation in some catchments.[3] Central government responded with policy programmes to address these water allocation issues; these are the focus of this chapter.[4] Thereafter, further policy programmes including the Land and Water Forum were developed.[5] Eventually, in 2011 the first national policy instrument to address water allocation was promulgated, the National Policy Statement Freshwater Management 2011.[6] These policy initiatives are now examined in further detail to measure their level of success in addressing New Zealand's water allocation problems. This chapter will argue that sufficient steps have not been taken to address water allocation problems that emerged during the policy gap. The starting point of this analysis is the Land and Water Forum.

The Land and Water Forum

The Land and Water Forum (the Forum) was the most promising and high profile water policy programme put forward by the government.[7] The Forum was established in 2008; it was based on collaborative governance principles to encourage participation in policy making from government and non-government stakeholders.[8] Collaborative governance is environmental decision making involving a broad range of stakeholders using processes that encourage a greater consensus between the parties.[9] The National-led government adopted a collaborative governance approach to water policy development after "increasing difficulty in establishing a consensus" across the government and non-government stakeholders involved in water policy development.[10] One of the barriers to establishing a consensus between parties was that "adversarial processes" were dominant in the administration of water permit and allocation processes.[11] The adversarial stance influenced the level and tone of initial mistrust amongst stakeholders.[12] The Forum began with building trust between the participants before embarking on policy development.[13] The Forum published recom-mendations in a series of reports discussed below. From a legal perspective, the Forum recommendations do not bind government because the Forum fell outside the processes for establishing "national direction" under the Resource Management Act (RMA).[14] The lack of legal status is a significant drawback of the Forum in terms of influencing changes to water management.

First Report of the Land and Water Forum – identifying problems with freshwater allocation

The First Report of the Land and Water Forum, A Fresh Start for Fresh Water (the First Report) focused on water law and policy problems stemming from a lack of national guidance and deficiencies in regional policy and planning.[15] For example, the First Report stated that there was an "absence of strategic process" in managing water and issues such as "agriculture, tourism, energy, biodiversity, landscape and land use".[16]

The lack of "strategic processes" can be traced back to New Zealand's institutional reforms of government departments responsible for water allocation during the 1980s. For example, two critical institutional changes occurred. First, the government divided water policy development across departments. It was divided as follows: The Ministry of Agriculture and Fisheries was responsible for irrigation water,[17] while the Department of Conservation had responsibility for freshwater fisheries[18] and the Ministry of the Environment had overall responsibility for national water policy development under the RMA. Second, national oversight was lost when the National Water and Soil Conservation Authority was abolished in 1988 and its functions regionalised to water boards.[19] Together, these two factors have led to the lack of strategic oversight as stated in the First Report because the national leadership in water allocation was lost.

The consequences of a lack of long-term hydrological data

The First Report stated there were "inconsistencies in our data collection, monitoring and analysis" stemming from the lack of hydrological information.[20] One of the causal factors was that "scientific research on water has fallen by about one third since the late 1990s" and "no single organisation is tasked with providing leadership" in this area.[21] Before the promulgation of the RMA, the National Water and Soil Conservation Authority collected national hydrological data.[22] Following the abolition of the National Water and Soil Conservation Authority in 1988, its water-related research functions were spread across eight Crown Research Institutes.[23] A competitive funding model diverted research resources away from the collection of long-term hydrological data resulting in a "smaller" hydrometric network "with a more variable distribution of sites, less commitment to QA and incomplete national archiving of data".[24] Problems also exist with measuring freshwater quality; moreover, the use of averages across different water bodies did not fairly represent the true state of water quality in New Zealand.[25] These gaps in water information contributed to a situation in which there is "no complete, up-to-date picture of what proportion of water bodies is allocated".[26] Ultimately, the scale of over-allocation across catchments is not known "and there is no clear baseline from which to measure future progress".[27]

The "first-in, first-served" rule and over-allocation

Recommendation 28 of the First Report of the Land and Water Forum stated that "economic opportunities are lost" due to the lack of direction in water allocation when applying the "first come, first served" method of allocation. Furthermore, "an absence of limits has resulted in a 'water rush' in some catchments as applicants seek more water than they need". The result is that combined with an "inflexible water permit transfer system" there is a reduction in water availability for "future uses". It continued by emphasising a lack of transparency in the lack of application of water allocation rules by councils in water permit application decision making. The "first-in, first-served" method of water allocation contributes to the problem of over-allocated catchments with calls that "A more flexible system for transferring water permits should be put in place only once over-allocation of water has been managed".[28] The First Report proposed changes; these included changes to conditions of consents as they expire so that consents are issued for a shorter duration, changing regional plan criteria for allocation decisions to include "efficiency and community consideration" or establishing a payment system for tendering or auctions of scarce water supplies.[29] The third option would mean significant changes to water allocation in New Zealand as it is essentially a recommendation for market-based water allocation.

Following the publication of the First Report, the government responded with a national direction on water policy and a significant commitment to funding irrigation projects. The purpose of the close examination of national policy here is to show that there was not a close alignment between the recommendations of the First Report and the national direction provided.

National Policy Statement for Freshwater Management 2014

In 2011, the National Policy Statement for Freshwater Management was promulgated. It was revised in 2014 and amended in 2017. Its statutory role is providing "national direction" on water policy issues relating to water quality and water allocation as follows.[30] Objectives B1 to B4 require regional councils to phase out over-allocation.[31] Policy B3 and B4 require regional councils to encourage efficient allocation and use. Objective B5 states communities can provide for their "economic well-being, including productive economic opportunities". Policy B6 is most relevant to over-allocation by requiring "every regional council [to] set [ting] a defined timeframe and methods in regional plans by which overallocation must be phased out".[32] The methods that may be used to phase out over-allocation include "reviewing water permits and consents to help ensure the total amount of water allocated in the freshwater management unit" does not exceed the limit or cap. However, these examples of "national direction" do not address the concerns raised in the First Report regarding the reallocation of water and easing the water transfer process. As a result, gaps remain in the national direction of water allocation law and policy in New Zealand at the highest level.

Funding for freshwater 'clean up' and irrigation after the First Report

The government established two funds following the Land and Water Forum's First Report. These funds were the Fresh Start for Freshwater Clean-Up Fund and the Irrigation Acceleration Fund (IAF).[33]

The purpose of the IAF was to support irrigation projects. The $35 million IAF was established on 1 July 2011 with the potential to increase to $400 million.[34] The IAF was projected to increase farm production on irrigated land in Canterbury, Otago and Marlborough by 64.1%, 12.2% and 6.8%, respectively. In comparison, the benefits to other regions were projected to range from 0.4% to 3.6%.[35] The projected benefits for Canterbury far outweighed those for any other region. The rationale for the IAF was the anticipated economic benefits of irrigation and the perception that private investors would not invest in irrigation schemes without government support.[36]

However, statistics refute the perception that privately funded irrigation was declining. Agricultural production statistics compiled by Statistics New Zealand showed that the total irrigated land increased significantly from 2007 to 2012.[37]

> The total irrigated land in New Zealand increased by 102,000 hectares between June 2007 and 2012, new information from the 2012 Agricultural Production Census shows. "Canterbury had the biggest increase in irrigated area, with an extra 60,000 hectares since 2007".

The justification of the IAF relied upon an economic analysis to support the need for a fund. Statistics on the growth of irrigation challenge the assertion that government-funded irrigation was necessary.

Furthermore, there was negligible support for irrigation funding for new dams in the First Report. It stated that the financing of irrigation schemes should ultimately be self-sufficient because "there is no magic bullet for financing rural water infrastructure projects that should sustain themselves on their own expected rate of return".[38] The report acknowledged problems with dam development and recommended policy changes focused on early collaboration to avoid the problems of "litigious and slow" dam development.[39] Improved allocation decisions were meant to create "new water" in rural infrastructure:[40]

> Improved rural infrastructure can provide a range of advantages for the economy, including through energy production and irrigation – and also for the environment. More reliable access to water can substantially increase primary production, including on dry-land farms. It can lead to more efficient and diverse use of water (higher value crops, for example) and reduce contamination of water bodies. It can produce energy savings and may allow the replenishment of aquifers and the restoration of streams.

Clearly, "improved" rural irrigation infrastructure is entirely different from the IAF funding proposals for building new dams. The IAF was also meant to improve energy production and irrigation in existing irrigation schemes.

Under the IAF, Crown Investment was limited to being a "minority partner" investing on "commercial terms".[41] Private investors would take over half of the risk in a proposed irrigation scheme. However, there were schemes where the public funding threshold of 50% was exceeded as local government bodies also began investing in IAF schemes. The Ruataniwha Water Storage Scheme provides an example of the limitation on public investment. The Hawkes Bay Regional Council (HBRC) wanted to invest

$80 million in the Ruataniwha Dam project, with the total cost estimated at $275 million.[42] Project success depended upon securing resource consents for the dam in its proposed form, including a land swap involving conservation land.[43] The Tukituki Catchment Proposal Board of Inquiry's Draft Report and Decision was issued on 15 April 2014.[44] It granted resource consents needed for the project to continue, subject to maintaining key water quality parameters.[45] As already noted, a land swap proposal involving conservation land was part of the scheme. The Department of Conservation had agreed to trade 22 hectares of the Ruahine Forest Park which had conservation park status. Initially, the land swap decision made by the Director-General of the Department of Conservation was upheld in the High Court.[46] However, in the Court of Appeal and Supreme Court, the High Court ruling was overturned by majority decisions.[47] In response to the ruling, the Hawkes Bay Regional Council decided to write off its investment in the scheme and not to proceed further.[48]

The end of state-funded irrigation

As discussed above, the IAF projects could be controversial political issues. Public interest in water issues and proposed irrigation schemes was also high. In the 2017 general election, water issues became one of the major voting concerns.[49] A water royalty was proposed by the Labour party, while the National opposed the royalty.[50] Farmers were particularly concerned about the possibility of a levy on their water use, with some farmers asserting that it might be an extra unaffordable cost.[51] In October 2017, upon coming to power, the Labour-led coalition government committed to ending irrigation funding. No further new agreements for irrigation schemes would be entered into and funded by Crown Irrigation Investments Limited.[52]

The Second and Third Reports of the Land and Water Forum

The Second Report of the Land and Water Forum focused on water quality issues while the Third Report focused on water allocation more specifically and how to transfer water to "highest value use" for the benefit of society.[53] Proposals for the strengthening of water rights were put forward in Recommendation 25 of the Third Report in order to improve the transfer of water permits.[54] The Third Report also stated that freshwater reallocation requires the establishment of "clear limits" to prevent over-allocation.[55] Limits would encourage users to be more efficient so that water is "set free" to allow further expansion, or "involve consideration of storage and other related infrastructure".[56]

155. A regime based on limits requires easily transferable water consents to allow users to make investment decisions and to adjust their use to maximise profitability. To achieve this, users' authorisations need to be clear, secure and enforced. This will support investment certainty and will allow users to manage more effectively within a limit. Clear, secure and enforced consents will also protect users from their entitlements being undermined by over-allocation.

These statements set out a pathway to improvements in water allocation that involve changes to property rights and methods of market-based water allocation.

Fourth Report of the Land and Water Forum – water markets

In November 2015, the Land and Water Forum published its Fourth Report. It stated that improving water transfers "is important for minimising the costs of reducing over-allocation" and for shifting water to "the best economic uses".[57] It recommended a cap on water allocations by setting extraction limits. This "limits based regime provides a framework that will allow markets to develop, and provide signals about when to invest in infrastructure" regarding investment viability.[58] Recommendation 57 addressed the issue of water markets for water allocation as follows:

Recommendation 57. The government should:

a) Monitor the emergence of markets for the transfer of water and discharge consents
b) Consider whether any market dominance or efficiency problems arise
c) Address them through the provisions of the Commerce Act where possible
d) Develop a specific response that targets the problems that arise if they are not able to be dealt with by the Commerce Act

While these statements are succinct, the policies and regulations required to implement water markets are complex. Recommendation 57 represents a clear indication that New Zealand's central government should consider how to implement water markets. The amendments to the National Policy Statement in 2017 did not specifically include a focus on water markets despite the recommendations to do so in the Fourth Report of the Land and Water Forum. As a result, the disconnect between the Land and Water Forum recommendations and national direction in government policy mean that gaps remain in addressing problems with New Zealand's water allocation framework.

National Policy Statement for Freshwater Management 2017 Amendments

Amendments to the National Policy Statement in 2017 can be traced back to 2016, that is to the Next Steps for Freshwater proposals.[59] The Next Steps for Freshwater public consultation document asked for public submissions on "technical efficiency standards" and "good management practice standards" (Proposal 2.5) to reduce over-allocation.[60] Proposal 2.4 in the Next Steps for Freshwater consultation document provided a range of options to improve water transfer including unbundling consents, establishing a public register of consents and "model plan provisions specifying where and in what circumstances transfers are permitted". The document then focused on the benefits of water transfers, rather than elaborating on methods to achieve those transfers.[61] The Submission Summary Report stated that Proposal 2.4 was based on recommendations from the Fourth Report.[62] The public submissions separating water take and use were split in terms of their support for or against the proposal. Some public submissions questioned the capability of the market to deliver on water transfers. There was general support for a public water register. While in general there was support for the use of markets to allocate water, submitters had reservations about pricing mechanisms and potential market failure.[63] Clearly, in this instance, the government has consulted on the establishment of water markets and some of the associated changes that would be required to implement change.

The Clean Water document issued in February 2017 then sought public submissions on proposed changes to the National Policy Statement.[64] Most of the changes addressed water quality issues. Objective B5 and Policy B8 discussed below were the key changes in the water quantity area. Amendments made in 2017 added Objective B5:

> Objective B5 To enable communities to provide for their economic well-being, including productive economic opportunities, in sustainably managing freshwater quantity, within limits

As a result, the 2017 Amendments to the National Policy Statement Freshwater Management do not address water allocation.

The Fifth Report of the Land and Water Forum

At the request of the Labour-led coalition government, the Fifth Report focused on specific issues related to water quality.[65] The report specifies the "steps members of the Land and Water Forum assert are needed to manage [water] within limits and avoid further degradation".[66] The focus of the

Fifth Report is to improve water quality. It stated that a Land and Water Commissioner office should be established to oversee the implementation of steps to improve water quality. A Land and Water Commissioner could also potentially have a role in implementing water allocation policy in the future. Overall, the Fifth Report makes a strong argument for greater direction at the national level.

Further environmental policy analysis with relevance to water allocation was released in 2019 by the Environmental Defence Society.[67] The Reform of the Resource Management System Synthesis Report provides a non-government analysis of environmental law and policy development in New Zealand. It proposes four different models for future environmental law reform. One of the models proposed includes the enactment of an Allocation Act that would include the allocation of water and other natural resources.[68] The difference would be that the allocation function of the RMA would be transferred to a new act.

National Policy Statement Freshwater Management implementation

Regional councils are still in the process of implementing the National Policy Statement Freshwater Management 2014.[69] Regional councils must give effect to National Policy Statements by implementing them in regional plans.[70] The National Policy Statement Freshwater Management 2014 has been referred to as relevant policy in the following cases. In *Li v Auckland Council*, the Court referred to the National Policy Statement as one of the relevant policies in determining that a rezoning application for land in the Okura catchment should be declined.[71] In *Pierau v Auckland Council*, an application to stage a music festival at Te Arai Point, a coastal area, was declined after taking into consideration statutory planning documents including The New Zealand Coastal Policy Statement 2010, the National Policy Statement Freshwater Management 2014, the *Hauraki Gulf Marine Park Act 2002* and relevant provisions of the regional and district plan.[72] The proposal was assessed under the National Policy Statement Freshwater Management 2014 to determine if there were any water quality issues; both parties agreed there were none.[73] The National Policy Statement Freshwater Management 2014 is at the top of the planning framework for determining applications relating to water quality. However, it has little policy guidance that is directly relevant to water allocation.[74] Furthermore, there are no cases which show the application of water allocation methods being affected by the national direction in the National Policy Statement Freshwater Management 2014.

Summary

The previous chapter examined the lack of guidance in water allocation, which created a water allocation policy gap for almost 20 years. This chapter argued that the government did not implement water policy recommendations from the Land and Water Forum Reports to address the problem of water allocation. While the work of the Land and Water Forum has influenced national direction on water management in the National Policy for Statement Freshwater Management 2014, the National Policy Statement has not gone far enough to address the issues that were raised. Other initiatives such as the funding for irrigation have been unsuccessful in providing an answer to the problems of increased demand and how to reallocate water. Clearly, gaps remain in the area of water allocation law and policy.

Currently, national policy direction does not provide a clear mandate for contemplating water markets or payment for access to water. In comparison, Australia has embraced water markets as a critical part of its water law reform. The Land and Water Forum Report recommendations which support the introduction of water markets to improve water allocation place New Zealand at a crossroads. For this reason, Australia is a prime example of how to implement water reform in terms of how to introduce markets and improve water allocation. New Zealand can learn from the Australian experience. To that end, the following chapter will examine how Australia dealt with its water scarcity problems by improving the ability to transfer water rights through water markets.

Notes

1 See Christina Robb *Water Allocation a Strategic Overview* (Ministry for the Environment, Wellington, 2001) which identified the problems with the lack of adequate regional planning for water allocation; Lincoln Environmental *Information on Water Allocation in New Zealand Report No 4375/1* (Ministry for the Environment, Wellington, 2000) for a more general discussion of water allocation issues; Department of Prime Minister and Cabinet *Sustainable Development for New Zealand Program of Action* (Department of Prime Minister and Cabinet, Wellington, 2003) for a policy programme for sustainable development in New Zealand which addressed freshwater allocation.

2 New Start for Freshwater Cabinet Paper at [16]. www.mfe.govt.nz/sites/default/files/new-start-for-fresh-water-paper.pdf

3 Cabinet Paper *Appendix 1 Background on Sustainable Water Program of Action in New Start for Freshwater* (n.d.) at 28 outlined the limitations of the "first come, first served" method of water allocation particularly in regions where there was increased competition for water.

4 The formation of "national direction" under the RMA can occur in the form of National Policy Statements, National Environmental Standards and the New Zealand Coastal Policy Statement. See Resource Management Act 1991, Part

5, Subpart I "National direction". In 2017, the Act was amended to introduce national planning templates. However, national planning templates have not been used yet to implement water allocation planning on a national level. An initial policy programme, the Sustainable Water Programme of Action (SWOPA), was released in 2004 with "extensive discussion" in 2005. Cabinet Paper *Appendix 1 Background on Sustainable Water Programme of Action in New Start for Freshwater* (n.d.).
Russell. M Fisher and Shona Russell "Water Policy and Regulatory Reform in New Zealand" (2011) 27(2) *International Journal of Water Resources Development* 387 at 388 noted the SWOPA was only able to develop some "soft options" for addressing water allocation issues in New Zealand; Andrew Hayward "Freshwater Management: Water Markets and Novel Pricing Regimes" (2006) 10 *NZJEL* 215 at 220 described the SWOPA as providing only "vague" proposals.

5 The Forum has produced five reports since 2008. Each of these reports is discussed in this chapter.

6 Central government guidance on the national direction for water allocation was contained in the National Policy Statement for Freshwater Management 2011. (Revised in 2014 and reviewed in 2017).

7 Ann L Brower "Is Collaboration Good for the Environment? Or, What's Wrong with the Land and Water Forum?" (2016) 40(3) *NZJE* 390. In 2018, the Labour coalition government asked the Land and Water Forum to prepare a fifth report to respond to water quality issues. Land and Water Forum *Land and Water Forum Advice on Improving Water Quality: preventing Degradation and Addressing Sediment and Nitrogen – May 2018* (Land and Water Forum, Wellington, 2018) at 4.

8 The policy programmes prior to the establishment of the Forum are detailed in the previous chapter Land and Water Forum *Terms of Reference for Land and Water Forum Project* (Land and Water Forum, Wellington, 2009). The Forum was established in 2008, initially under the name the Sustainable Land Use Forum, as part of the New Start for Freshwater Programme and later renamed the Land and Water Forum; Guy Salmon and others (2008) "Collaborative governance on environmental policies affecting rural land owners: comparing Nordic and New Zealand practices" paper presented at the Yale University UNITAR conference on environmental governance.

9 Elizabeth Eppel "Collaborative Governance Case Studies: The Land and Water Forum" (2013) Working Paper 13/05 Institute for Governance and Policy Studies, School of Government, Victoria University of Wellington at 27.

10 Above.

11 Melissa Robson and others "The Collaboration Lab: The Transformative Role of Collaboration in Managing our Land and Water" in L.D. Currie and M.J. Hedley (eds) *Scient and policy: nutrient management challenges for the next generation. Occasional report No. 30.* (Fertilizer and Lime Research Centre, Massey University, Palmerston North) at 2.

12 Eppel, above n 9, at 7.

13 Above.

14 Resource Management Act 1991, Part 5, Subpart I "National direction".

15 Land and Water Forum *Report of the Land and Water Forum: A Fresh Start for Fresh Water* (Land and Water Trust, Wellington, 2010) at vi.

16 At viii.

17 Ministry of Works and Development Abolition Act 1988.
18 Conservation Act 1986, section 6(ab). Section 6(ab) was inserted, on 10 April 1990, by HYPERLINK "http://www.legislation.govt.nz/act/public/1987/00 65/76.0/link.aspx?id=DLM207989" section 4 of the Conservation Law Reform Act 1990. The Conservation Law Reform Act 1990 also established the New Zealand Fish and Game Council.
19 Water and Soil Conservation Amendment Act 1988.
20 First Report of the Land and Water Forum, above n 16, at viii.
21 Above.
22 Water and Soil Conservation Act 1967 section 14(k).
23 AD Fenemor, T Davie and S Markham "Hydrological Information in Water Law and Policy: New Zealand's Devolved Approach to Water Management" in J Wallace and P Wouters (eds). *Hydrology and Water Law Bridging the Gap* (London, IWA Publishing) at 11.
24 At 11.
25 Mike Joy (2014, June). *The Demise of New Zealand's Freshwater; Politics and Science*. At Hamilton Branch of the Royal Society. Also presented at Christchurch Branch of the Royal Society; Wanaka Branch of the Royal Society; Invercargill Branch of the Royal Society and Rotorua Branch of the Royal Society.
26 Cabinet Economic Growth and Infrastructure Committee "Implementing the New Start for Fresh Water: Proposed Officials' Work Programme" (n.d.).
27 Above.
28 Land and Water Forum Report of the Land and Water Forum: A Fresh Start for Fresh Water, above n 15, at 3.
29 Land and Water Forum, above n 15, at xi.
30 Resource Management Act 1991, sections 45–55.
31 Policy B1 requires implementing the National Policy Statement by having regard to climate change and connections between water bodies. Under Policy B2, regional councils making or amending regional plans should ensure they "provide for the efficient allocation of fresh water to activities, within the limits set to give effect to Policy B1".
32 The National Policy Statement for Freshwater Management 2014 also requires addressing over-allocation to manage water quality too. National Policy Statement for Freshwater Management 2014 (Amended 2017) at 5.
33 Land and Water Forum Second Report of the Land and Water Forum. Setting Limits for Water Quality and Quantity (Land and Water Trust, Wellington, 2012) at xii; For access to policy documents leading to the implementation of the Clean Up Fund and the Irrigation Acceleration Fund see the Ministry of Environment (2014) Funded projects for Fresh Start for Fresh Water Clean-up Fund www. mfe.govt.nz/issues/water/freshwater/fresh-start-for-fresh-water/cleanup-fund .html
34 Office of the Minister for the Environment. Office of the Minister of Agriculture *Fresh Start for Fresh Water. – High Level Government Response to the Land and Water Forum Report* CAB; David Carter 9 May, 2011 Budget 2011: Lifting investment in irrigation www.beehive.govt.nz/release/budget-2011-lifting-in vestment-irrigation
35 NZ Institute of Economic Research Inc and AgFirst Consultants NZ Ltd *Value of irrigation in New Zealand: An Economy-wide Assessment Final Report to the Ministry for Primary Industries* (Ministry for Primary Industries, Wellington, 2014) at 8.

36 Above.
37 Statistics New Zealand (2013) "Big increase in irrigated land supports more agricultural production" *Agricultural Production Statistics: June 2012* (final) – Media Release.
38 First Report of the Land and Water Forum, above n 16, at 42.
39 Land and Water Forum Report, above n 16, at ix.
40 At xii.
41 Ministry for Primary Industries *Irrigation Acceleration Fund (IAF) Guidelines for Applicants* (Ministry for Primary Industries, Wellington, 2010) at 8.
42 Hawkes Bay Regional Council Ruataniwha Water Scheme HB Today Public Meeting 6 August 2015 at slide 13. Available at www.hbrc.govt.nz/assets/D ocument-Library/RWSS-Documents/Ruataniwha-slides-6-August-public-meeting.pdf
43 Deloitte Peer Review of the Ruataniwha Water Storage Scheme Business Case (Hawkes Bay Regional Council, May 2014).
44 Radio New Zealand "Final dam submission decided by officials" *Radio New Zealand News* (17 September 2013).
45 Board of Inquiry into the Tukituki Catchment Proposal Final Report and Decision of the Board of Inquiry into the Tukituki Catchment Proposal in Relation to Matters Referred Back by the High Court June 2015.
46 *Royal Forest and Bird Protection Society of New Zealand Inc v Minister of Conservation* [2016] NZHC 220, (2016) 19 ELRNZ 370.
47 *Royal Forest and Bird Protection Society of New Zealand Inc v Minister of Conservation* [2016] NZCA 411, [2016] 3 NZLR 828; *Royal Forest and Bird Protection Society of New Zealand Inc v Minister of Conservation* [2017] NZSC 106.
48 Simon Hendery "Council writes off $14m investment in failed Ruataniwha dam project" *NZ Farmer* (30 August 2017).
49 Charlie Mitchell "Political parties sense opportunity on water issues" *Stuff NZ* (14 July 2017).
50 Nicole Sharp "Election 2017: Water royalty point of divergence" *Otago Daily Times* (8 September 2017); Patrick Gower "Public, politicians divided over water tax" *Newshub* (7 September 2017).
51 Anusha Bradley "Pressure on Labour's water tax" *RadioNZ* (13 September 2017).
52 Labour, New Zealand First, New Zealand Labour Party & New Zealand First Coalition Agreement 52nd Parliament (2017).
53 Land and Water Forum *Second Report of the Land and Water Forum. Setting Limits for Water Quality and Quantity* (Land and Water Trust, Wellington, 2012); Land and Water Forum *Third Report of the Land and Water Forum: Managing Water Quality and Allocating Water* (Land and Water Trust, Wellington, 2012) at 36.
54 At 36. Recommendation 25 states "The design of the allocation system should remove administrative barriers to transfer and trading".
55 At 95. 2. Initial allocation will be important in some under-allocated catchments, and where new water is created. However, it is likely that many catchments will be fully- or over-allocated once all use is accounted for within the allocable quantum. The goal of achieving efficiency in the allocation regime in this case will focus on the ability for the water to move between uses over time.
56 At 95.

57 Land and Water Forum *Fourth Report of the Land and Water Forum* (Land and Water Forum Trust, Wellington, 2015) at x.
58 Above at [92]. Ministry for the Environment *Next steps for fresh water: Summary of submissions*. (Wellington: Ministry for the Environment). ME1248 June 2016 at 4.
59 The 2017 Amendments were preceded by the Clean Start for Freshwater policy programme undertaken in 2016.
60 At 25.
61 At 24. Enabling such transfers will increase incentives for existing users to invest in efficiency improvements beyond those specified in the technical efficiency standards, and transfer excess water or discharge allowances to others. It will also provide incentives for existing users to temporarily transfer water or discharge allowances if they do not need them for a while. Doing so would increase the economic value that we get from the available resource.
62 At 27. The proposals were originally built on recommendations presented by LAWF in the group's third and fourth reports. Recommendation 25 from LAWF's third report stated that "water … needs to be easily transferable between users, to allow it to move to its highest valued use … The design of the allocation system should remove administrative barriers to transfer and trading". The discussion of this recommendation also describes that consents should be standardised, making provisions for trading these consents. LAWF's fourth report also discusses how to facilitate transfers, saying that lack of access to information creates a barrier to transfers.
63 At 28.
64 Ministry for the Environment *Clean Water 90% of Rivers and Lakes Swimmable by 2040* (Ministry for the Environment, Wellington, 2017) ME1293.
65 Land and Water Forum *Land and Water Forum Advice on Improving Water Quality: preventing Degradation and Addressing Sediment and Nitrogen – May 2018* (Land and Water Forum, Wellington, 2018) at 4.
66 At 1.
67 Greg Severinsen and Raewyn Peart *Reform of the Resource Management System The Next Generation Synthesis Report* (Environmental Defence Society, Auckland, 2019).
68 At 21.
69 Regional councils that have not already implemented the National Policy Statement Freshwater Management 2014 were required to prepare implementation plans. See Ministry for the Environment *National Policy Statement for Freshwater Management Implementation Review: National Themes Report* (Ministry for the Environment, Wellington, 2017). See also Ministry for the Environment *Briefing for the Incoming Minister; Water* (Ministry for the Environment, Wellington, 2017) at 10 states "That there has been some public criticism that progress has been slow in some regions".
70 *Environmental Defence Society Incorporated v New Zealand King Salmon Co Ltd* [2014] NZSC 38.
71 *Li v Auckland Council* [2018] NZEnvC 87.
72 *Pierau v Auckland Council* [2017] NZEnvC 90.
73 At [50].
74 See *Hokio Trusts v Manawatu-Wanganui Regional Council* [2017] NZHC 1355 [2017] NZRMA 543; *Eyre Community Environmental Safety Society Inc*

v Christchurch Regional Council [2016] NZEnvC 178 was focused on dam safety management, not water allocation; *Sustainable Matata v Whakatane District Council* [2016] NZEnvC 16; *Creswick Valley Residents Association Inc v Wellington City Council* [2015] NZEnvC 149 stated that the National Policy Statement Freshwater Management 2014 was a relevant consideration when addressing the issue of water contamination from earthworks but there was no evidence presented on the Policy Statement.

4 Australian water allocation law and policy

Introduction

This chapter analyses Australian water allocation law and policy. Australia has undertaken extensive and complex water law reform in the last 20 years. An analysis of constitutional powers shows the Commonwealth lacked overt authority to allocate water. Thus, it had to rely upon other constitutional powers to implement water law reform. Ultimately, the lack of a clear constitutional authority led to tensions between the states and the Commonwealth. Hence, the implementation of water reform across all states was hindered by the constitutional structure. The critical evaluation in this chapter supports the view that due to constitutional issues, progress in water allocation law and policy implementation was initially rather slow.

The incentive for change began during the 1970s and 1980s when Australia's water allocation problems gained international attention. The Commonwealth responded by formulating water policy objectives at the Council of Australian Governments (COAG) meeting in 1994. The meeting was a milestone for water law reform as all Australian states began to work collectively to address water allocation problems. Following the 1994 COAG meeting, the National Water Initiative 2004 supported the adoption of water markets for water allocation in the form of a cap and trade model. The objectives of the National Water Initiative 2004 were implemented in The Water Act 2007 (Cth). The water allocation law reform experience is critically evaluated from a legal perspective. There is a strong case to address the relevant legal issues before embarking upon extensive water market law reform. More recently, concerns have also been raised about the water law reform by academics and practitioners questioning the effectiveness and implementation of the Water Act 2007 (Cth).[1] Amongst other matters, there is concern that the measures undertaken as part of reform, such as buying back water from irrigators, has not delivered the amount of water that would improve the health of the Basin.

Finally, the implementation of the Water Act 2007 (Cth) and the Murray-Darling Basin Plan are analysed in the states of Victoria, New South Wales, South Australia, Queensland and Western Australia. It shows the regulatory processes followed in each state to implement law reform. The analysis of how the Act has been implemented is core to the comparative analysis in the next chapter.

Water policy development in the Murray-Darling Basin

Water and the drafting of the Australian Constitution

One of the "legacies" of colonial water policy is that the states "continue to hold sway over national water policy formulation today".[2] Indeed, it is true that states continue to dominate the policy development at the national level. The discussion that follows reflects the legacy of colonial water policy as it was then, and remains today, closely tied to the economic output of each state. Within this policy context, the states must ensure that they do not push their demand for water beyond environmental limits. How the states balance their own demand for water against each other and the environment is reflected in the constitutional tug-of-war over water allocation issues.

The drafting of the Australian Constitution raised concerns about the availability of water and the potential effect on individual colonies. Following the Federation Drought of 1895–1902, water would have been a high priority for colonies. The high status of water resources was reflected in the fact that the topic of water was debated for weeks.[3] The debate addressed how existing rights may be affected in relation to navigation and irrigation if a Commonwealth government was formed. State access to water for irrigation was crucial for development and states were reluctant to relinquish control of water resources to the Commonwealth. The final concessions made by the states are clearly stated in the Australian Constitution 1901.

The states kept as much control as possible over the use of water resources. The Australian Constitution only directly refers to water or natural resources in sections 98 and 100.[4] Section 98 of the Australian Constitution states:

> The power of the Parliament to make laws with respect to trade and commerce extends to navigation and shipping, and to railways the property of any State.

Section 100 states:

> The Commonwealth shall not, by any law or regulation of trade or commerce, abridge the right of a State or of the residents therein to the reasonable use of the water of rivers for conservation or irrigation.

Section 98 extends the scope of section 51(i) with regards to trade and commerce to include navigable rivers and rail. Section 100 was included to appease states' concerns about the extent of Commonwealth power over navigable rivers.[5] The states were concerned about the growing importance of irrigation and whether section 98 of the Constitution could override state interest in other uses of water.[6] Their concerns were unfounded. As the use of rivers changed from navigation to irrigation, the power under section 98 became irrelevant.[7] The states retained a great deal of control over water resources. The Commonwealth did not have direct power to implement water allocation policy across Australia.

Indigenous Australians have been excluded from water law and policy development because the legal recognition of indigenous rights did not occur until the 1990s.[8] The decision in *Mabo v Queensland* confirmed the indigenous rights of Aboriginals to land and water were not abolished by the colonial acquisition of sovereignty and could be recognised in common law.[9] The Murray-Darling Basin Authority provided guidance on the inclusion of indigenous communities in water planning.[10] There has been a slow progression in the inclusion of indigenous values in water planning. In 2009, the National Water Commission reported that indigenous communities were rarely included in water planning.[11] Consultation with indigenous communities has improved, however, there remains more work to be included in indigenous communities in water allocation strategy.[12]

Early water-sharing agreements between states

Tension has existed between federal and state systems of allocating water from the time of Australian colonies. There is "long-standing tensions between the two layers of government that go much wider than water policy and management".[13] This tension has been most evident in the Murray-Darling River catchment.[14] There are many communities and farms dependent on water in the Basin.[15] The Basin contains 65% of irrigated land in Australia and produces 39% of total agricultural production.[16] Consequently, the greatest demand for Basin water is from irrigation.[17] Tension arises from the Basin being an important source of agricultural production and the need to balance this with environmental, cultural and social factors too.[18]

Prior to the more recent water law reforms, there were earlier attempts to address this tension by encouraging greater cooperation between the Basin states.[19] The River Murray Waters Agreement (RMWA) 1914 between New South Wales, Victoria and South Australia resulted in the creation of the River Murray Commission in 1917 (RMC), which would oversee the water sharing agreement.[20] The RMC managed water sharing (and the associated costs) between states in the Murray-Darling Basin.[21] The Agreement focused on the development of infrastructure for water storage when it was promulgated.[22] One shortfall of the Commission was that its commissioners acted in the interest of the state governments that appointed them.[23] Balancing the collective needs of the Murray-Darling Basin catchment and individual state interests remains one of the problems facing water allocation law and policy in Australia.

The state-sponsored construction of dams

The state commitment to the RMWA was put under pressure by developments which increased demand for water. The time period from 1917 to the early 1970s saw the expansion of Australian water infrastructure.[24] In particular, the development of further irrigation infrastructure increased the demand for water in Australia.[25] Unfortunately, irrigation investment after World War II was based on erroneous environmental assumptions about soil and hydrology.[26] These irrigation schemes lacked regulatory guidance,[27] and the financial viability of irrigation schemes was also an issue. Private investors often initiated irrigation schemes, but public funds were spent on water supply infrastructure.[28] During the 1940s some states cooperated to construct large dams.[29] The downside of this construction was that water allocation within these schemes became increasingly complex to manage. There was broad discretion in the application of administrative criteria for managing the dams.[30] The dams became oversubscribed and dam managers exercised their discretion when making complex water decisions during water shortages.[31] These factors led to problems with over-allocation within the larger schemes.

Evidence of over-allocation in the Murray-Darling catchment

The failure of the existing water sharing agreements between states (such as the RMWA) became apparent as more evidence of over-allocation in the Basin emerged. Over-allocation became increasingly apparent in the 1970s and 1980s as the Murray-Darling catchment began to show the environmental effects of over-allocation.[32] By the early 1980s, the pressure from growing development and demand for water in the Basin contributed to the failure of the RMWA.[33] In response, the River Murray Commission, which was established as part of the RMWA, was also replaced[34] by the Murray-Darling Basin Ministerial Council, the Community Advisory Committee and the Murray-Darling Basin Commission.

Commonwealth utilisation of 'external affairs' power

The Commonwealth government responded to over-allocation by encouraging increased co-operation between the states within its limited formal powers under the Constitution.[35] This section begins by discussing the Commonwealth heads of power in the Constitution.[36] The Commonwealth government faced the problem of coordinating a response to over-allocation, within the constitutional framework. The policy response was needed to cover state and natural catchment boundaries. The Tasmanian Dam case discussed below is relevant to understanding the use of Constitutional power to address environmental issues. The analysis in this section shows that the lack of a clear constitutional mandate at a Commonwealth level has been a problem in Australian water allocation law.

Australian water law reform at the Commonwealth level relied upon the implementation of international law through the "external affairs" power in section 51(xxix).[37] It was used to implement international treaties and agreements into domestic law. The "external affairs" power is defined in broad terms and as a result "the range of topics the Commonwealth can regulate via the external affairs power has expanded considerably".[38] The expansion of the external affairs power includes international agreements such as the World Heritage Convention signed in 1974 and the Ramsar Convention signed in 1975.[39]

The Ramsar Convention required signatories to identify and list significant wetlands. These wetlands must then be protected to encourage their "wise use" as stated in Article 3 of the Convention. The implementation of the Convention has been through the provision of the Basin Plan discussed below. The legal requirement to implement the Convention is in section 20(a) of the Water Act 2007 (Cth), which requires the Act to give effect to "relevant international agreements". Failure to give effect to international agreements would violate the Basin Plan itself in accordance with constitutional law.[40]

The World Heritage Committee accepted nominations of heritage sites from each government. In Australia, this was the Commonwealth government. The implementation of the Convention was subject to political debate and created divisions between Commonwealth and state level governments as they pursued the green vote.[41] The Tasmanian Dam case was a high-profile case which illustrated these political tensions and how they raised constitutional points of law. In particular, the legal question was whether the Commonwealth government had power to rely upon its "external affairs" constitutional power to implement international environmental conventions within states.

"External affairs" power and the Tasmanian Dam case[42]

The Hydro-Electric Commission of Tasmania followed a policy of "hydro-industrialisation" to improve state development.[43] In 1967, the Commission proposed the first stage of a dam which included flooding Lake Pedder. This proposal was met with strong public resistance.[44] However, the first stage was constructed. In 1979, the Hydron-Electric Commission tabled the second part of its dam proposal for the Franklin River. Again, there was public resistance to the proposal. In 1983, the incoming Commonwealth government pledged to stop dam construction if elected.[45] It passed the World Heritage Properties Conservation Act 1983 (Cth) overriding state power to approve the dam project.[46] The Act was based on the Convention Concerning the Protection of the World Cultural and Natural Heritage, which was ratified by Australia in 1974.[47] In passing the Act, the Commonwealth relied upon section 51 (xxvi) to make rules for people "of any race, for whom it is deemed necessary to make special laws" and the power to govern "external affairs" under section 51 (xxix) of the Constitution. Before the Tasmanian Dam case, the extent of the Commonwealth's external affairs power was unclear.[48] The Tasmanian Dam case confirmed the wide powers of the Commonwealth.[49] Further decisions also confirmed the "external affairs" power and its use to implement international treaties.[50]

The legal status of the Commonwealth government to implement water law reform was reviewed early in the reform process. The Senate Legal and Constitutional Affairs References Committee confirmed that greater transparency was required on the development of water law reform. With regards to the exercise of constitutional power by the Commonwealth government, it stated:[51]

4.11 The committee agrees that the ambiguities in the provisions of the Water Act, in relation to the development of the Basin Plan, have largely resulted from the absence of a clear constitutional power for the Commonwealth over water regulation in Australia. In the committee's view, the basis upon which the Water Act is established is unsound: there are clear question marks over the adequacy of the constitutional heads of power (namely, the external affairs power), as well as the limited state referral powers, upon which the Act relies.

The lack of clear constitutional power and its effect on the law reform process are detailed in the section below which evaluates the implementation of the Water Act 2007 (Cth) and the creation of the Murray-Darling Basin Plan. However, there is also a sense that the legal basis of water law reform is closely tied to political factors.

There is strong evidence to suggest that drought also drives the development water reform policy. Many studies link the law reform initiatives in Australia to preceding droughts.[52] The current water reforms "have their parallels to reform in the early twentieth century" as both reform processes had to respond to extreme droughts.[53] The common factor is that in drought conditions states are more willing to cooperate on water policy.[54] During the 1990s, drought and evidence of further environmental problems in the Murray-Darling catchment showed that more urgent action was needed to address over-allocation. During the "Millennium Drought" from 1997–2009, precipitation in Australia was recorded at its lowest level since 1900s.[55] Prior to the Millennium Drought, drought was considered a "climatic abnormality" from a policy perspective and responses to drought were managed as part of disaster relief policies and funds.[56] However, the use of disaster relief policy soon changed with the longer drought, issues with the drought support payments and the perception that the government should develop a strategic response to the problem of droughts that were extreme.[57]

The Millennium Drought placed the Commonwealth government under pressure to respond to water allocation in a coordinated manner. A strong policy response was required to address the problems with water allocation exacerbated by drought. The Millennium Drought was so severe that individual state responses alone could not solve the water allocation problems of the Murray-Darling Basin.[58] Under drought conditions, states were more willing to work together to address water allocation problems. Water policy implementation had to start at the Commonwealth level down to state and regional levels.[59] This approach was different from the previous efforts to address water allocation problems through water sharing agreements, as described above.

Despite the severity of drought, the Commonwealth government remained reluctant to make full use of its external affairs power as upheld in the Tasmanian Dam case. Instead, it opted to follow a policy of "cooperative federalism", which meant working with states to implement environmental policy.[60] On the one hand, cooperative federalism may have been a tactical response to gain state support to implement much needed water reform.[61] However, on the other hand, consensus between states was critical to ensure the progress of such extensive environmental reform. Cooperative federalism was better for the long-term success of implementing water allocation law reform because it established a foundation of mutual respect and trust.

The COAG Water Reform Framework 1994 and "cooperative federalism"

In 1993, the COAG commissioned The Working Group Report on Water Resources Policy to investigate water resource problems.[62] The Report stated problems existed in the water industry with the unsustainable use of water, inefficient service delivery, inadequate provision for upgrading infrastructure in rural areas, barriers to moving water to higher-value uses and the need for clarity around the role of water industry institutions.[63] The Working Group Report on Water Resources Policy recommendations were incorporated into the COAG Water Reform Framework 1994.[64]

Another critical factor influencing Australia's water law and policy reform was concurrent competition policy reform. An Independent Committee of Inquiry examined the National Competition Policy in 1993, resulting in National Competition Reforms.[65] The committee focused on developing a national competition policy in areas where traditionally the public sector had maintained ownership and control, and was critical of public monopolies such as in the gas, electricity and water industries.[66] The National Competition Reforms drove the changes to water markets. States were given three "tranche" payments to meet obligations relating to implementing gas, electricity and water reforms.[67]

The COAG Water Reform Framework 1994 objectives

The COAG Water Reform Framework 1994 objectives stated that a Water Framework was required to ensure "an efficient and sustainable water industry". The framework should include pricing, based upon "full-cost recovery", and future water schemes should be assessed for their economic and ecological sustainability. Unbundling of property rights was also a significant objective as it would change how water entitlements were defined.[68] Further objectives related to establishing an Environmental Water Holder, addressing over-allocation and establishing water markets.

The significance of the National Competition Reforms in the context of water reform was that it emphasised the market value of water. These market-based concepts were reflected in water policy and vice versa; water policy was included in the competition policy. For example, the COAG Water Reform Framework 1994 objectives were incorporated into the 1995 National Competition Policy agreements.[69] States were required to implement water, competition and other policy as required. The competition reforms supported the marketisation of water. Hussey and Dovers state the importance of competition reform as follows:[70]

> National Competition Policy drove reform in many policy domains, and the "Council of Australian Governments water reform" of the 1990s, were a leading example. These reforms focused on productivity, reduction of state subsidies, user-pays, separation of policy and provision, privatization and corporatization of functions, break-up to allow competition, use of market and property right mechanisms and importantly provision of flows to the environment.

The competition reform context provided an additional level of account-ability too as state progress in implementing the reforms was monitored.[71]

The establishment of the National Water Commission

A commitment to water markets – The National Water Initiative

The 1994 COAG reforms and Water Reform Framework 1994 indicated a change in water policy towards greater use of markets for reallocation. However, obstacles to the establishment of water markets included political opposition from those holding existing allocations and the complexity of regulating market rules for trading water.[72] Institutional changes were required to overcome these problems.[73] The establishment of the National Water Commission in 2004 was one of the most important policy contributions of the National Water Initiative.[74]

There had also been greater emphasis on surface water rights in the past. The National Water Initiative (NWI) addressed the imbalance by providing for the recognition and planning for groundwater at the same level as surface water in clause 23(x).

A further issue affecting the implementation of market-based water allocation was "the complexity of current water property rights".[75] Australia's historical water allocation policy had resulted in different licences, permits and irrigation rights to water between states, which needed to be addressed as part of reform.[76] One of the first steps to achieve standardised water policy was in the COAG Water Framework 1994 and NWI, which both stated that water rights should be unbundled.[77] In order to facilitate unbundling, states were encouraged to follow the NWI directive to separate water property rights from land. It did not prescribe the method for states to unbundle. As a result, there are different types of water property entitlements across states. Unbundling was controversial because it "marked a significant change in the governance of water as a common pool resource within Australia".[78]

The significance of a water cap on water extraction

The implementation of a cap on water extraction was an important step in addressing the over-allocation problem in the Murray-Darling Basin. The cap was also critical in establishing water markets in Australia because it indicated the catchment was fully allocated.[79] The process of establishing a cap on water extraction from the Basin began with the Murray-Darling Ministerial Council limiting surface water diversion in 1995 in response to over-allocation.[80] At first the cap was temporary. It became a permanent cap in July 1997. On one hand, the cap is viewed positively as the most important decision of the Ministerial Council because all states agreed to it voluntarily.[81]

However, on the other hand, there was criticism that the cap would not be an effective policy to address over-allocation because the extraction limits were based only on prior use when they should have been based on sustainable limits that took into account environmental needs.[82] Connell concludes the cap failed because it was not fully implemented.[83] The cap depended on states to implement it in order for it to be successful; however, the Commonwealth had no legal mandate for "states to resource the necessary compliance work".[84] In support of his position, he gives the example of the cap not being extended to include groundwater, even though there was a policy to do so. Connell contends that the failure of the cap was symptomatic of the "general failure" of the Murray-Darling Ministerial Council to implement policy to improve the environmental health of the Basin.[85] By the early 2000s, there was growing concern that the initial momentum in water policy from the early 1990s was declining.

The voluntary cap transitioned into mandatory sustainable limits under the Water Act 2007 (Cth). It required the establishment of "environmentally sustainable limits" as part of the Basin Plan.[86] The policy incentives for capping surface water diversions were to improve the overall environmental health of the Murray-Darling River Basin and encourage water trading.[87] The move to mandatory sustainable limits was part of a broader Commonwealth response to encourage states to renew their commitments to advancing water policy. The provisions of the Water Act 2007 (Cth) reflect a desire to make improvements to the allocation of water in the Basin. It introduced a range of new policy measures that states were required to implement in accordance with the Act.

The Water Act 2007 (Cth) required states to legally recognise the environment as a water user.[88] In this regard, Australia is a leader in water policy development. Environmental water is not a feature of New Zealand water law. Comparative studies on water law show there is a "greater acceptance" of the concept of environmental water by the Australian government than other countries, such as America.[89]

Commonwealth water law and policy – The Water Act 2007 (Cth)

The Commonwealth's national policy programme included the enactment of the Water Act 2007.[90] The regulation and implementation of Australian water reforms deserves closer attention and the Water Act 2007 (Cth) is central to the recent reforms.[91] The Water Act 2007 (Cth) regulates water allocation in the national rather than state interest. In doing so, it takes a top-down approach to implementing the reforms. From a constitutional perspective, the Act gives effect to international agreements, while reducing over-allocation and protecting ecological values.[92] The objects of the Act emphasise economic interests, water security and cost-effective policy development. These objects form the basis of the Commonwealth's direction to states on water allocation law and policy development. The enactment of the Water Act 2007 (Cth) was to revive state commitment and interest in implementing the water law reforms initiated in the early 1990s.

Sustainable diversion limits

The Basin Plan limits water extraction through the establishment of sustainable diversion limits in Part 2 of the Act. Water resource plans within the catchment must be accredited by the Murray-Darling Basin Authority as evidence that they comply with the Act. The Basin Plan must identify critical human water needs and how to meet them. The regulation is focused on the future with practical requirements to consider growing demand from increased populations. Limitations in the scope of the Basin Plan mean that it only controls the management, allocation and trading of water. It does not control land use. Section 22(10) states that the Basin Plan has "no effect" on land use planning or the "control of pollution". The Basin Plan focuses on water allocation issues, not water quality and land use planning. The limitations on land use planning is a point of distinction compared to the New Zealand situation.

Sustainable diversion limits aim to increase the volume of environmental water to the Basin. The methods to reach the sustainable diversion limits have divided opinions on whether the right balance is achieved between human consumptive needs and environmental needs. In particular, there are concerns that the sustainable diversion limits should be reformed to include consideration of climate change.[93] Returning water to the Basin is contentious because of this "trade-off" between competing demands for water, as discussed below.[94]

The return of 2750 GL to the environment

An important question in the formulation of the Basin Plan is how much water is needed to restore the Basin health. Estimates of how much water needs to be returned to the Basin has changed over time. For example, research undertaken by the Wentworth group stated 4350 GL were required to be returned to the Basin for a good chance of success in restoring its environmental health.[95] In 2010, the Wentworth group provided a further detailed report stating that 4400 GL was the volume needed to restore the health of the Basin.[96] In 2010, the Murray-Darling Basin Authority also provided a figure to restore Basin health, which differed from the Wentworth Group. It stated 3860 GL were needed for there to be a reasonable likelihood of success in restoring the health of the Basin. Upon releasing this figure to the public in the first Basin Plan, there was shock from the irrigation community as it realised the degree of change that was needed to restore Basin health.[97] Once sustainable diversion limits included social and environmental impacts, the final figure of targeted water to return to the Basin environment in 2012 was 2750 GL. There was a lack of transparency in determining this final figure and a Senate Inquiry into the management of the Murray-Darling Basin Authority in 2013 recommended that a transparent explanation of the 2750 GL figure should be given to the public.[98] A further problem with the 2750 GL figure is that it only applies to surface water and there has been a fivefold rise in the volume of groundwater extraction.[99] In 2017, the Murray-Darling Basin Authority proposed revising the sustainable diversion limit.[100] The consultation Draft Determination Report stated that the Basin was on track to meet its target of 2750 GL of water being recovered annually on average and effectively 605 GL less water needed to be diverted to the environment. The basis for the determination was that the Authority was overseeing a number of projects that would deliver the 605 GL to the environment. The decision of the Authority in changing the sustainable diversion limits is highly questionable. In particular, the scientific basis of the Authority's Draft Determination Report was criticised in the South Australian Royal Commission into the Murray-Darling Basin Plan.[101]

In addition, in 2012 the Commonwealth government added a commitment of 450 GL to also be returned to the environment, which was agreed to by Basin states in 2018.[102] The 450 GL was subject to ensuring that socioeconomic criteria were met before returning the water to the environment.[103] It shows the ongoing tension between balancing the needs of water for the environment and the community. The criteria state that projects must be made public, that they should not have a negative effect on social or environmental outcomes and there should be clear timing for project completion. Of greater importance to the achievement of 450 GL, environmental water return are the criteria relating to irrigation. For example, criteria 6 states:

> Programs or projects do not have negative third party impacts on the irrigation system, water market or regional communities
>
> a. Where a proposed project is located within an irrigation network, the proponent must provide evidence that the relevant network operator or water corporation is involved in or aware of the project.

b. The relevant government or proponent must consult industry bodies, irrigation network operators, local governments or regional development organisations, on a strategic regional approach which will focus on ensuring there is a mix of water efficiency projects in a region in ways that address industry, network/system and local/regional priorities, future needs and risks and may include research and extension services.

c. The socio-economic assessment of programs or projects must consider impacts not just on participants, but for broader regions

The requirements under criteria 6 and other criteria requiring consultation with community and industry leaders ensure that there are actual water savings and to consider how to make existing projects more efficient will be challenging to navigate. The extra criteria from the Ministerial Council challenge the legal basis of the Water Act 2007 (Cth) and the Commonwealth's power to implement its water allocation policy across states in a systematic manner. The criteria is damaging to the Commonwealth and state collaboration that has been undertaken for Australia to develop its Basin Plan in the first place.

The setting of sustainable diversion limits are subject to extensive complexity. The complexity arises not only from developing proper policy but also political interests.

Water buy-backs

One of the methods for meeting sustainable diversion limits has been through water buy-backs by the government. In the Murray-Darling Basin, the Australian government has undertaken the "world's biggest buy-back of water rights" costing approximately $2.5 billion Australian dollars.[104] The buy-backs generally occurred through the government purchasing water allocations by entering the water market.[105] Water buy-backs were meant to assist with improving the environmental health of the Basin. However, it has been difficult to measure the direct correlation between water entitlement buy-backs and the health of the Basin.[106] Water buy-backs have been the most contentious issue for the rural community.[107] There were strong protests against the perceived effect of buy-backs on the rural economies where buy-backs occur.[108] It is unlikely that further buy-backs will occur.[109]

Instead, government policy has shifted towards acquiring environmental water by investing in infrastructure improvements to save environmental water.[110] But now the shift towards investing in infrastructure is subject to criticism from a number of academics who question the policy on a number of grounds.[111]

An alternative non-government approach to water buy-backs is the Murray-Darling Basin Balanced Water Fund.[112] The Fund was established by the Nature Conservancy on a "counter cyclical" basis so that at times of scarcity more water is allocated to irrigators and in times when there is more water available it is allocated to wetlands.[113]

Establishment of the Commonwealth Environmental Water Holder

As the Basin Plan is implemented, there is an increasing amount of environmental water being returned to the Basin's natural environment. The administration of environmental water was carefully considered during the National Water Initiative and Living Murray policy programme. As a result of these policy programmes, the Water Act 2007 (Cth) established the Commonwealth Environmental Water Holder (CEWH) to be the repository of environmental water management. The CEWH is responsible for managing water acquired through water buy-backs and improvements to water infrastructure.

The legal status of environmental water in the water market is the same as an irrigator. O'Donnell's research on the role of environmental water managers such as the Commonwealth Environmental Water Holder has provided interesting insight into their roles.[114] The research was based on interviews with staff at a range of environmental water bodies which had separate legal personality. Her findings confirmed that the role of the environmental water managers was constrained by their own interpretation of their rights and ability to be the "voice" of environmental water. In fact, the environmental water managers were unlikely to see their legal personhood as an opportunity to advocate for the environment in this manner. The role of environmental water managers was perceived as one where they were to deliver water to the environment, much like irrigators. O'Donnell stated that this interpretation of environmental water manager powers potentially prejudiced the ability of the environment to have an advocate for environmental water as Parliament intended.

Water charges

The Act regulates water charges. Water charge rules are legislative instruments which may be created by the Minister under Part 4, Division 1, section 92(2). Anti-competitive behaviour within the markets is addressed by the Australian Competition and Consumer Commission (ACCC). Section 99 states that the ACCC monitors and enforces the water market rules. The Minister for the Environment must consult the ACCC before making any rules.[115]

Water charges and compliance issues related to market rules, under Part 4 and Part 4A of the Act, are monitored by the ACCC. Section 94 requires the ACCC to monitor and report on compliance with the water market rules. Section 137 reinforces the distinction between the market compliance function of the ACCC and the functions of the Murray-Darling Basin Water Authority. In comparison, the Authority is responsible for the enforcement of matters contained in Part 2 of the Act. Part 2 of the Act relates to water management issues. The institutional split follows the market-based method of water allocation. For example, the higher-level management of water remains with the Authority. It is the role of the Authority to prepare the Murray-Darling Basin Plan as required by the Water Act 2007 (Cth). Unlike New Zealand, the institutional split of water for irrigation is not at the highest level of water management. Water allocation policy is developed in an integrated manner. The Authority prepares the Basin Plan in consultation with Basin states, the Basin officials committee, the Basin Community Committee and the ACCC.

New Zealand does not have policy or laws regarding the establishment of water markets, the definition of rights for water products and the role of the Commerce Commission in water market. These issues will be considered in detail in the next chapter.

Property in water entitlements – *ICM Agriculture v The Commonwealth*

The implementation of the water reforms at the state level have resulted in legal issues on constitutional points of law. This case provided an opportunity for the High Court of Australia to examine the legal basis for water allocation by the government.[116] In particular, from a constitutional perspective, the decision contributed to the understanding of the acquisition of property under "just terms" in section 51(xxxi). The acquisition of property under just terms has a strong legal foundation.[117] Four main requirements must be considered when determining whether section 51(xxxi) applies. First, whether what is acquired by the Commonwealth is classified as "property". Second, whether the property has been acquired. Third, if the property has been acquired the compensation provided is on "just terms". Fourth, the property has been acquired for a reason supported by the Commonwealth's power to make laws in that particular area.[118] The first point was accepted in this decision. The second point on whether there had been an acquisition of property was the most pertinent in the case.

ICM Agriculture Pty Ltd (ICM) was an Australian agricultural company. It challenged the replacement of its existing water rights with a water licence under the Water Management Act 2000 (NSW). The New South

Wales government was changing the previous groundwater bore licences that had initially been issued under the Water Act 1912 (NSW). The change effectively reduced the amount of water available to ICM. ICM was offered "structural adjustment payments" by the state acting through the National Water Commission.[119] The Schedule of the Water Management Act 2000 required the preparation of Water Sharing Plans. The effect of the Water Sharing Plans was to reduce water entitlements over ten years.[120] The Funding Agreement was entered into by the National Water Commission on behalf of the Commonwealth.[121] ICM argued that the payment amounts were inadequate and they "would not amount to 'just terms' within the meaning of section 51(xxxi) of the Constitution".[122] The majority judgment accepted the point that the State should not acquire property other than on "just terms". This conclusion led to further examination of further legal issues. The Court then had to consider whether the change in the plaintiffs bore licence involved an acquisition of property other than on just terms within the meaning of section 51(xxxi).[123]

The plaintiffs argued that their existing bore licences issued under the Water Act 1912 (NSW) were property. The Court considered the reliance on arguments based on English common law. It drew attention to the replacement of the riparian doctrine by the Irrigation Act 1886 (Vic) because the riparian system did not cope well with the water scarcity experienced in the Australian climate. States used legislative power to vest the ownership of water with the Crown.[124] The importance of recognising the effect of these earlier Acts was that they vested the right to use and control water with the Crown.[125] The vesting of water with the Crown had implications for the issue of whether or not property had been acquired on just terms.

The Court held that the change to the water right was not an acquisition of property. It disagreed with the plaintiffs, who argued that the "property" they had acquired in their bore licences under the Water Act 1912 (NSW) had been eroded. The Court was effectively asked to consider whether those statutory water entitlements resulted in the creation of property.[126] Then, if there was an element of property, whether this had been acquired by the State when it replaced the bore licences issued under the Water Act 1912 (NSW).

The Court held that the granting of a bore licence issued under the Water Act 1912 (NSW) and its replacement with water entitlements under the Water Management Act 2000 was not an "acquisition" of property by the State. The reasoning of the Court was based on the following assertions. First, the physical nature of groundwater makes it a public resource, which meant the State did not gain anything from limiting the use of water.[127] Second, since 1966, a licence was required for the right to take water:[128]

The rights the plaintiffs had under their bore licences (in particular, their right to extract certain volumes of water) did not in any sense "return" to the State upon cancellation of the licences. The State gained no larger or different right itself to extract or permit others to extract water from that system.

The remaining justices observed that the plaintiffs were not arguing about the erosion of a "private right enjoyed by them". The plaintiffs were arguing about access to a natural resource, which the "State always had the power to limit the volume of water being taken from that resource".[129] The judicial reasoning focused on the fact that "there was no acquisition of property". The State itself had not gained anything through the action of replacing bore licences. Fisher observes the strong position of the State in managing common resources on behalf of the community as follows:[130]

> The State was and always had been – certainly under the arrangements by which the State exercises it exclusive right to use and control of water resources – able to control the use of water resource as the common resources or common property of the community. This had probably been the position under the common law and certainly was the position under the legislation.

Fisher provides an important observation — particularly the fact that the underlying position of the common law was, in reality, the vesting of water in the State as a common resource. The starting point for a discussion on the nature of property in a water entitlement should be to acknowledge the status of water as a common resource.[131] This decision set a strong precedent for other licence holders in New South Wales. The decision confirmed that the government could reduce entitlements without it being an acquisition of property, which would have otherwise triggered the requirement for "just compensation".

Water accounting

The valuing of water as has been undertaken as part of water reform in Australia requires reliable measurement and accounting.[132] The National Water Initiative required states to implement water accounting.[133] The purpose of water accounting was to facilitate benchmarking to create consolidated water accounts on state and national levels.[134] To achieve the objective of comparable water accounts, the water accounting system needed to be standardised. Standardised water accounts were important because it would allow a comparison of water accounts to measure compliance with water entitlements and contribute to water trading information.[135]

In the Australian context, water accounts also had wider constitutional implications. As described above, each state was required to implement water law reform under the Water Act 2007 (Cth) and reduce water allocation to sustainable limits. Compliance with sustainable limits of water allocation and the calculation of water savings needed to be measured in a comparable manner. As will be discussed later in this chapter, concerns in states such as New South Wales about water takes and the effect on downstream states has become an issue for the success of the National Water Initiative 2004. Ultimately, it is the perception of the integrity of water accounting systems, which is important for state support of water reforms. States need to be able to rely upon water accounting information to compare and measure their performance in collectively moving towards improving the health of the Murray-Darling Basin.

Specific provisions relating to environmental water accounting are also included. Environmental water is recorded in a register which includes information on "source, location, volume, security, use, environmental outcomes sought and type".[136] Environmental water as defined in paragraph 35 is given the same legal status and security as other water entitlements.[137] The Australian water accounting system includes environmental water as part of its accounts.

Water accounting standards form the foundation for water accounting in Australia. In 2006, the National Water Accounting Development project established water accounting as a discipline.[138] The Water Accounting Standards Boards was established to guide the development of Australian Water Accounting Standards.[139] It included experts from the fields of financial accounting, water management and policy.[140] In 2009, the Water Accounting Standards Board published the Water Accounting Conceptual Framework.[141] The Conceptual Framework informed the creation of the Australian Water Accounting Standards. It recognised concepts relating to the creation of water assets and liabilities for a water entity in order to prepare accounts showing changes in the use of water. The Conceptual Framework stated that a "water entity" was not defined in legislation:

12. Legislation does not define the concept of a water report entity; nor does it prescribe who shall prepare general purpose water accounting reports in most cases. However, the Water Act 2007 requires the Bureau of Meteorology (Bureau) to compile and maintain water accounts for Australia, including a set of water accounts to be known as the National Water Account even though the Bureau is not directly responsible for national water management and distribution. This requirement demonstrates that the preparer of general purpose water accounting reports does not need to be the water report entity for which those water

accounting reports are prepared. This is most obvious where the water entity is physical in nature.

The water reporting entity could be an "irrigator" or an "environmental water holder".[142]

The communication of water information in the form of water accounts was a significant conceptual and practical progression from considering such information as hydrological data. The users of water information vary, and the Conceptual Framework emphasised standards and a standardised language that would allow different stakeholders in the water industry to communicate more effectively with each other. Water information is not just for water management. It is also needed by those who participate in water markets. States implementing water reforms rely on having comparable water accounting standards to measure and report on progress on their water reform processes.

Summary of Commonwealth water law and policy reform

As we have seen, assessments of the Australian water reforms by academics and practitioners state that the reforms have been successful in addressing a number of problems that were facing Australian water allocation, but further improvements can be made.

Australia has addressed constitutional barriers to implementing water law reform. The Water Initiative 2004 and the Water Act 2007 (Cth) have been central to the reform process and the establishment of water allocation through a market-based system. Market-based water allocation has improved the ability to respond to droughts in a more flexible manner as the transfer of a range of water products creates another asset for businesses. There is evidence that markets have assisted with the "resilience" of agricultural enterprise in Australia and water trading has had a positive effect on the regional GDP of states in the Basin.[143]

However, the regulation of markets is an ongoing point of contention during the water reform process. Regulation includes both compliance and enforcement. Regulation of water markets should improve equity and efficiency for the environment. At a regional level, the lack of compliance has been linked to a lack of water market participant knowledge of the importance of compliance limits.[144] Increased monitoring of water licences could assist in preventing unintended effects of a lack of compliance with water market regulation.[145]

The following section examines how the requirements of the Water Act 2007 (Cth) have been implemented in states. Effectively, it is the compliance aspect of the regulations which could undermine the water law reform process that the Commonwealth has undertaken. Details such as accurate metering are required at the state level to ensure that water theft does not occur. Hence, it appears that the accurate monitoring of water information relates to the integrity of the water market.

A further issue at the state level is the regional impact of water trading. For example, in some catchments there may be more trade out of a catchment than is desired by the community. Markets do not address wider social concerns and impacts on communities.[146] Nor do they always deliver the environmental outcomes that are desired. Markets may still allow people to acquire a windfall gain. Finally, the water markets do not operate "equally" or in a standardised manner across Australia. The lack of standardised market practices in turn affect the cap and trade system of market implementation. The implementation of national water allocation law and policy at the state level is not uniform. The differences between states can be "profound" because of "the legacy of ostensibly independent state control".[147] These differences are evident in the evaluation of how the National Water Initiative 2004 and the Water Act 2007 (Cth) were implemented at the state level.

Water allocation law in Victoria

As we have seen, each state was required to implement the water reforms. The state of Victoria is a leader in implementing water reforms that "most fully replicates the goals of the National Water Initiative".[148] The system of creating new water products varied according to the reliability of supply, level of supply and duration and was described as part of the unbundling process by Godden, who also described the Victorian response to the National Water Initiative as "a best practice model".[149] The Water Act 1989 (Vic) is the primary source of water law in Victoria. The Act sets out the requirements for water allocation, water trading and the creation of sustainable water management plans. Water allocation categories in the Act are distinguished as bulk entitlements, environmental entitlements, water shares and water licences. A further significant development in Victoria was the establishment of the office of the Environmental Water Holder. While the previous section outlined the key aspects of water law in the Australian Commonwealth, this section will detail water allocation in the state of Victoria focusing on the Water Act 1989 (Vic).

Statutory framework – Water Act 1989 (Vic)

The purpose section of the Water Act 1989 (Vic) focuses on the problem of over-allocation and water management.[150] The Act provides "for integrated management of all elements of the terrestrial phase of the water cycle". Hence, integrated water management acknowledges the water cycle, and not just freshwater in a lake or underground. Section 1(c) requires the "orderly, equitable and efficient" use of water, which connotes a level of management required across the state. Section 1(d) requires water to be "properly managed for sustainable use for the benefit of present and future Victorians".

Unbundling

As part of the unbundling of water rights, distinctions were made between the right to take, use water and the delivery of water. An irrigator must hold a water use licence before it can take water for irrigation.[151] A water licence will record the details of the licence holder, a description of the land specified in the licence, any conditions on the licence and when the licence is valid.[152] The purpose of the licensing system is to reduce the adverse effects of irrigation on unsuitable land by controlling where irrigation can occur. The adverse effects include reducing the effects of salinity, managing groundwater infiltration, protecting biodiversity and reducing the cumulative effects of water use.[153] Delivery licences are also attached to the land but are separate from use licences. They allow for the delivery of water to an irrigation area.[154] A delivery licence will give a degree of security to a landowner regarding the ability to have water delivered through infrastructure at times of high demand. Delivery shares are tied to the land.

"Water shares" determine the amount of water that can be taken from a "declared water system".[155] These systems are commonly water storage dams for irrigation. A "water share authorises the taking of water under the water allocation for the share during the season for which the water allocation is allowed".[156] A water share will specify the location and rate at which water is taken.[157] Section 33S allows the transfer of water shares to another user.[158] Section 33T allows for the partial or full transfer of a water share for a fixed period. Section 33U allows for the assignment of the full water share or a part of it to any person. Water shares are recorded on the water register and may be sold, mortgaged or leased. The water register is essential to provide accurate information to water market participants.

Bulk water entitlements (major water takes)

The Act effectively provides the framework for various water products. The transfer of water products is often the focus in the literature of water markets, but it is important to acknowledge that it is regulation which defines rights in accessing water within a market.[159] Bulk entitlements are defined in section 34(1)(a) as any water corporation holding licences for "water

supply or irrigation", a person holding a water licence, an electricity generation company or Minister for Conservation and Forest Lands.[160] The bulk
entitlement may be held by a company, the Environmental Water Holder or
another body. Applications for bulk entitlements are made to the Minister
for Environment, Climate Change and Water who must take into account
matters as outlined in section 40.[161] The Minister may consider "the purpose for which the water is to be used" and "the needs of other potential
applicants".[162] The matters outlined in section 40 are broad and do allow
the Minister to look at hydrological factors and "any other matter that the
Minister thinks fit to have regard to".[163] It is significant that the Minister
for Environment, Climate Change and Water may consider other information related to the current application to judge whether the application is
approved.

Once granted, bulk entitlements may be defined according to volume,
stream flow or a share of the volume or stream flow.[164] Bulk entitlements
measured as a share of storage should include the method for calculating
the entitlement. Bulk entitlement from another Authority must detail situations where the water supply can be discontinued, or reduced, as allowed
under section 141 of the Water Act 1989 (Vic). The bulk entitlement may
specify the "obligations of the storage manager, the resources manager and
the environmental manager" associated with the bulk entitlement holder,
which can include decisions about releasing flows for the environment.[165]
The bulk entitlement can record information in relation to whether it can be
transferred and any financial obligations of the Water Authority which holds
the bulk entitlement.[166] The bulk entitlement may state the water accounting methods and whether credits are available to the Authority if water is
returned to the water source. The conditions that may be specified with a
bulk entitlement under section 43, as described above, provide the Minister
for Environment, Climate Change and Water with statutory power to ensure
that compliance with other water policies in water management, allocation
and reporting are met by the bulk entitlement holder.

Victorian water register

The Victorian water register contains the details of water-related entitlements and allocations of water in declared and non-declared systems.[167]
The purpose of the water register is to "facilitate reporting in relation to
records and information about water related entitlements" and provide public records about ownership and use of those entitlements.[168] The Minister
is responsible for "establishing and maintaining" the Water Register. The
water register records water-use licences, water-use registrations, bulk entitlements, environmental entitlements (as described below), the amount of

water allocated to water shares in declared systems and works licences.[169] Details recorded regarding water shares include the class of reliability of the share. Information regarding the transfer of water shares in section 84J is supplemented by Market Rules which provide further guidance such as identification requirements for individuals applying to transfer water shares.[170] The water register is available online.[171]

The Victorian Environmental Water

Allocations for environmental water have been changed to "environmental entitlements" so that environmental water is on par with other water entitlements in the water market.[172] This specific allocation for environmental water needs goes beyond relying upon the maintenance of minimum flow levels alone. Environmental water in the state of Victoria is held by the Environmental Water Holder (Water Holder), which is a separate body corporate independent of any department. An application for environmental water may be made by the Minister or the Water Holder.[173] Environmental water in Victoria was previously held by the Victorian Department of Sustainability and Environment (DSE). O'Donnell's review of the Victorian Environmental Water Holder details three key factors, or policy drivers, influencing the establishment of the office of the Victorian Environmental Water Holder as an independent office.[174] First, the increased "propertization of water rights [which] began with the *Water Act 1989* establishing tradable water rights".[175] The propertisation of water rights influenced the need to allocate water to the environment in order to participate in the water market. The creation of environmental water rights was based on the premise that water is a public good and "poorly adapted to participate in the market based system that allocates clear property rights to private goods".[176] This point was also recognised at the Commonwealth level by the NWI. The second policy driver was to improve the management outcomes of a larger pool of environmental water to be held together by the Water Holder. The third, and most influential policy driver, was the challenges posed to the concept of environmental water during the extreme drought Victoria experienced from 2006 to 2009. The drought and its challenge to the idea of environmental water deserves closer scrutiny.

Environmental water at times of scarcity

Decisions about water allocation during the drought showed the subordinate position of environmental water compared to other water uses. In particular, it illustrated the conflict of interest of government departments when allocating water in times of extreme scarcity. For example, the Victorian

Minister for Water had the power to declare a water shortage and "qualify any rights to water whether or not they relate to the same area".[177] The term "qualify" is defined as "suspend, reduce, increase and otherwise alter".[178] O'Donnell states the effect of the Minister for Water qualifying 12 river basins effectively reduced the environmental flows.[179]

> In a democratic society, it is probably generally accepted that the role of the Minister for Environment is to present a balanced overall perspective from the Government on environmental matters. However, when that Minister holds environmental water, the question arises as to whether the Minister for Environment can represent environmental interests and concerns fairly?

At the time of low water flow, the Minister stated that the environment "needed to shoulder some of the burden during drought years" and more water should be allocated for consumptive use.[180] At that time, the Yarra River was at 35% of its normal flow.[181] The Environmental Defenders Office of Victoria (EDO), a non-governmental organisation, reported on the potential to reform the environmental water reserve in light of the perceived conflict of interest.[182] The EDO stated that despite water reform, "environmental water in Victoria is still of insufficient volume and not properly accounted for, and the majority of it is not a secure entitlement".[183]

The environmental water reserve improved the legal framework for environmental water, however, it had "fallen short of expectation and the needs of the environment, particularly in light of climate change".[184] The Environmental Defenders Office recommended that environmental water should be converted to "environmental entitlements" to place environmental water on equal grounds with consumptive entitlements. Also, the ability to reduce environmental entitlements should be subject to a transparent process that included public notification. It submitted that it was important for the office of the Victorian Environmental Water Holder to remain independent from the government in exercising powers to manage environmental water. The Report was critical of the lack of alignment with earlier policy objectives identified in the 2004 White Paper on Victoria's water law reform to improve outcomes for environmental water.[185]

The statutory role of the Victorian Environmental Water Holder

In response to the problems regarding environmental water, as described above, the Victorian government established an environmental water holder in 2010. The Victorian Environmental Water Holder (Water Holder) is a separate body corporate with "perpetual succession" and powers to "sue and be sued in its corporate name".[186] The Water Holder usually has three Commissioners with experience in environmental management, sustainable water management, economics or public administration.[187] If the Minister recommends that a Commissioner should be removed for not fulfilling their duties, then reasons must be provided to the House of Parliament within five sitting days.[188] This removal process assists in maintaining transparency in the appointment and removal of the Water Commissioners. Division 4 of the Act outlines the accountability of the Water Holder to the government. The Minister may give written directions to the Water Holder but must not direct the particular use of water. By distinguishing the independence of the Water Holder, a higher level of accountability exists to improve the outcomes for environmental water. The Water Holder must actively plan how it will act to meet objectives in the next financial year.[189] This "corporate plan" should detail the governance, functions and reporting of the Water Holder.[190] The Minister retains discretion over the contents of the Water Holder's corporate plan by having the legal ability to direct changes "to vary the plan as the environment Minister thinks fit".[191]

Environmental water and the water market

The Environmental Water Holder is a participant in the water market and has a public trading strategy.[192] It is important to note that section 33DE states that the "Water Holder has the power to do all things necessary or convenient to be done for, or in connection with" their duties. However, there is no further specific guidance on the matters that the Water Holder should consider when making decisions under the Act. For example, the Water Holder can sell water, but high volume sales could have a disproportionate effect on the water market. In announcing a recent sale of water, the Commission stated: "We have assessed current market conditions and adopted an implementation plan aimed at being a good corporate citizen, including by avoiding any significant adverse impacts on the market".[193] The requirements to consider the adverse effects on the market are not explicitly contained within the Water Act 1989 (Vic). At the same time, the Water Holder has been criticised for not having the legal ability to sell excess water each season to irrigators.[194] The Act requires that the money received from the sale of excess water is to meet the objectives of the Water Holder in section 33DC. Section 33DC states that the Water Holder should act to maintain environmental water and improve the overall health and condition of environmental water. These are broad objectives. A Liberal MP, Dr Sharman Stone, has advocated for the Water Holder to do more with proceeds from the sale of environmental water, other than making further purchases of environmental water. Examples of other use of the proceeds from the sale of environmental water include paying for the cost of storing environmental water in dams, which is estimated to be $25 million.[195] These more recent concerns about the management of environmental water suggest further changes may occur and that the water allocation policy will continue to develop in response to new challenges.

New South Wales water law and policy

The role of irrigation

New South Wales has a range of natural and regulated surface (released from dams) water.[196] Its experience of water law reform is important because most of the water is used for irrigation.[197] In comparison to Victoria, the water allocation rules in New South Wales "provide a relatively lower reliability of supply in many river valleys than in any other states".[198] Problems with New South Wales implementation of water reforms were stated as early as 2005 when the National Competition Commission assessed state progress on implementing a range of competition reforms, which included the water reforms. It raised concerns about the assessment of environmental water and whether it was based on the best scientific evidence.[199]

The process of privatising irrigation schemes

There were significant institutional changes in the water sector in New South Wales. Before the water law reforms, irrigation schemes were owned by the public sector. The amount of water available in an irrigation scheme depended upon the administrative decision making of the State. The proposal to privatise irrigation schemes raised concerns about the legal structure of new private institutions and how access to water would be defined. The privatisation of irrigation schemes was driven primarily by irrigators.[200] Privatisation was a two-step process of consolidating the existing schemes into five schemes before transferring them into private ownership models through the Irrigation Corporations Act 1994 (NSW). Division 3 of the Act was very systematic in providing a statutory basis for the transfer of assets and the negotiations that would precede the transfer.[201] The Irrigation Corporations Act 1994 was repealed on 1 January 2001 by the Water Management Act 2000 (NSW). Core provisions relating to the operation of Irrigation Corporations are now included in Chapter 4 of the Water Management Act 2000 (NSW).[202]

There are several critical elements in the privatisation process that New South Wales undertook, and New Zealand did not. These points are summarised in the work of Taylor and others.[203] The NSW government retained its regulatory oversight of private irrigation schemes in order to maintain the social and economic goals of the schemes and to ensure that the use of water was in the State interest. The regulatory oversight included measures to protect irrigators' rights following privatisation. The New South Wales government wanted to limit its exposure to the future costs of maintaining irrigation schemes. It would step back from its role in the daily administration and delivery of water. Maintaining the financial viability of the schemes would be in the hands of the new irrigation companies. Finally, the New South Wales government wanted to ensure the long-term sustainability of the privatised irrigation schemes. In comparison, New Zealand did not maintain regulatory oversight of its irrigation schemes once they were privatised under the Irrigation Schemes Act 1990.

Land and Water Management Plans were a part of the water licensing requirements of the irrigation schemes in New South Wales. Plans were to be prepared with the irrigation community, with government assistance and funding to implement the plans in the long term. The Land and Water Management Plan provided the government with ongoing policy oversight on the operation of the irrigation scheme. The New South Wales government did not step back from irrigation schemes as emphatically as New Zealand did in 1990.[204] The New South Wales approach to privatising irrigation schemes was much more systematic in its implementation.

Statutory framework – Water Management Act 2000 (NSW)

The Water Management Act 2000 (NSW) was promulgated as the primary legislation governing the management and allocation of water to implement the COAG reforms.[205] There is an important reference to the "cumulative impacts of water management licences and approvals and other activities on water sources and their dependent ecosystems" in section 5(d). The inclusion of cumulative effects of licences is important. The section maintains a focus on the environment and how the environment may be affected by the granting of several licences. Again, this is something that does not feature in New Zealand water allocation statutory requirements. The remaining subsections in section 5 focus on cultural, social and economic aspects of water. Overall, the principles contained in section 5 of the Act capture the critical water management issues faced by New South Wales. These objectives and principles influence how the Act defines water rights. The Water Management Act 2000 (NSW) abolished common law rights to water.[206]

The principles of the Water Management Act 2000 (NSW) and the Murray-Darling Basin Agreement are implemented through a State Water Management Outcomes Plan.[207] The State Plan will ensure that sustainable diversion limits are met as required under the Murray-Darling Basin Agreement.

Unbundling and water licences

Section 56 of the Act states the features of a "water access licence". It allows the holder access to a "share component" to take water at specified times and locations. The share component as stated in section 56(2) may be fixed at a maximum volume, a proportion of water or storage capacity, a specific proportion of dam inflow or a specific number of units. The "water access licence" may be assigned to a category of licence as stated in section 57(1), ranging from different levels of security to separate categories for larger takes such as local water utilities.

The different categories of water access licences reflect the degree of security in accessing the various water categories and also their distinctive characteristics. Section 58 states the priority between water licence categories. It prioritises "local water utility access licences, major utility access licences and domestic and stock access licences" over other access licences.[208] The duration of a water access licence is perpetual under section 69. Initially, water access licences had a duration of 15 years with major utilities having a licence duration of 20 years.[209] It also allowed licence holders to apply for a renewal of their existing licence within 12 months of the licence expiring. These original provisions were not in accordance with the National Water Initiative 2004 objective to strengthen water rights. The change to effectively perpetual ownership does not mean that there is a guarantee to a fixed amount of water being delivered. The water access right ensures access to an annual share of water, which may fluctuate. It is also important to note that the Minister may impose further conditions upon the water access licence holder under section 67. This also indicates that although the holder of the licence may have perpetual ownership, their licence remains a licence subject to the Crown being able to exercise its power to manage the underlying water resource in the future.

Environmental water in New South Wales

New South Wales is required to account for environmental water. It has taken a different approach from Victoria as it has not consolidated environmental water under a State Environmental Water Holder. Instead, New South Wales manages "planned" environmental water in water sharing plans and "Held" environmental water in environmental water licences.[210] The Plans will determine how water is shared between consumptive users and the environment. The underlying purpose of the Plans is to meet the requirements of states under the Murray-Darling Basin Plan.

New South Wales' progress on meeting the environmental water targets has been heavily criticised in the Murray-Darling Basin Authority's December 2018 progress report.[211] The progress report states that New South Wales is "behind schedule" with 20 plans under development. It concedes that the state is making an effort to invest in water planning. It is currently operating under old plans, which includes the Barwon-Darling Plan that has been subject to criticism following the media attention from the 2017 ABC Four Corners programme alleging that water theft was occurring unchecked.[212] Following the programme, the New South Wales Department of Industry responded to the concerns that had been raised. In their response, the Department emphasised that they were working on a new set of water plans that would be accredited. Of greater significance was the written confirmation that the Department had spoken to irrigators about "walking away" from the water reforms:[213]

> Have you ever discussed with irrigators and/or their representatives plans for NSW to walk away from the Murray Darling Basin Plan?
>
> Yes – it is prudent for the NSW Government to consider all possible scenarios for the implementation of the Basin Plan, and to ensure the best possible outcome is achieved for NSW irrigators, the environment and regional communities.
>
> While NSW has considered alternative scenarios, we have also publicly advocated the benefits of the Basin Plan in its current form. In particular, we have explained to stakeholder groups the importance of seeing the plan through.

The legal ramifications of the investigation by the ABC Four Corners Program was a Royal Commission into the alleged allegations of water theft by South Australia.[214] The Royal Commission found serious problems with the administration of water confirming that the constitutional barriers could undermine state cooperation in implementing the reforms. The Native fish stocks in New South Wales have also been dying in the region in large numbers, indicating that surface water flows are at dangerous levels.[215]

Water law and policy in South Australia

Statutory framework

The Natural Resources Act 2004 (SA) is the primary legislation affecting water allocation in South Australia. Plans for water management and allocation are a core part of the Natural Resources Act 2004 (SA). The state of South Australia is divided into eight regions which each have their own

Natural Resources Management (NRM) Boards.[216] Within each region, "A regional NRM board may, by notice in the Gazette, designate an area within its region as an area within which an NRM group will operate".[217] The Board appoints the Natural Resources Management Group members.

Section 48 of the Natural Resources Management Act 2004 (SA) requires that the NRM Group composition include up to seven members with collective "knowledge, skills and experience" to meet the Group's obligations. The process for appointing the Board is a form of "government assisted self-organisation".[218]

The selection process for Group members "must" include public notice asking for expressions of interest.[219] The appointments are subject to consultation with the relevant council, Primary Producers SA Inc and the Conservation Council of South Australia.[220] Section 52 states the function of Natural Resource Management Groups. Section 52(1)(a) requires the Group "to be actively involved in the development and implementation of any relevant regional NRM plan at the local level". It is also required to educate the community on the "importance of integrated and sustainable natural resources management" and provide advice to the regional NRM Boards.

The NRM Group is an integral part of managing natural resources in South Australia by being involved in the creation of natural resource management plans. The Board appointment process reflects the top-down approach of the water reforms. There is concern that this approach may decrease local capacity to respond to drought because some legitimacy has been lost in the process of removing the pre-existing governance bodies.[221]

Unbundling and water licences

Water licences issued under the Water Management Act 2004 (SA) provide for an ongoing right to take water. Water licences can provide for a "water access entitlement", which specifies the volume of water that can be taken.[222] Water for personal domestic or household use does not require a licence, which includes water for domestic stock.[223] Under section 146(2), a "water access entitlement" gives access to a share of water from a "consumptive pool" to the licence holder subject to the Ministers' determination regarding how much water is available under section 146(3).

The Irrigation Act 2009 (SA) regulates water for irrigation purposes. It defines the irrigation water rights and basic requirements for irrigation trusts. Irrigation trusts hold the water right on behalf of the irrigators. It is a statutory requirement under section 29 of the Act to fix the amount of water that each member holds by having regard to the type of crops grown and any other relevant matters. Such provisions relating to the nature of crops grown on land are not included in New Zealand. The rights held by irrigators in an irrigation trust under the Irrigation Act 2009 (SA) may be converted to a water licence under the Water Management Act 2005.[224]

Natural Resource Management Plans

The Department of Environment, Water and Natural Resources must prepare a State Natural Resources Management Plan. The State Plan is required to demonstrate how the overall "objects" of the Natural Resources Management Act 2004 (SA) will be achieved.[225] The State Plan contains policy that guides the creation of further regional plans by NRM Boards:[226]

> At the centre of the NRM system is the State NRM Plan which provides the strategic blueprint for NRM boards and agencies to develop their own specific plans.

NRM Boards are required to prepare Regional Natural Resource Management Plans including the methods that will be used to improve the health of natural resources, conservation and land drainage issues.[227]

The NRM Board is also required to prepare a separate Water Allocation Plan for "prescribed" water resource in their region. Under section 76(4), it must include an assessment of the quantity and quality of water needed by the ecosystems.

These statutory requirements for a water allocation plan ensures a level of comparability across the Water Allocation Plans. The Plans should address issues relating to water quality and quantity, and if a water take has a detrimental effect on water quality that should also be taken into account. There is limited scope for the NRM Boards to avoid addressing the issues that are stipulated under the Act.

Water Allocation Plans that cover the Murray-Darling Basin located in South Australia must meet the requirements of the Basin Plan. The objects of the River Murray Act 2003 (SA) contained in section 6 stress the importance of using "all reasonable and practicable measures" to ensure that the River Murray is protected and restored. It also requires developing "mechanisms" to protect the River Murray "while at the same time providing for the economic, social and physical wellbeing of the community".

Water law and policy in Western Australia

Statutory framework

In 2005, Western Australia was the "only jurisdiction to have significant outstanding obligations on water industry legislation".[228] Western Australia responded to the changes required under the 1994 COAG Agreement by amending the Rights in Water and Irrigation Act 1914 (WA) in the year 2000.[229] The amendments allowed the unbundling of water licences so that they could be traded separately from land. The take and use of water is subject to obtaining a licence under the Rights in Water and Irrigation Act 1914 (WA). The Western Australian approach was to add to the existing water law framework. This type of water allocation and licensing follows a "traditional approach".[230] This traditional type of entitlement is generally a fixed entitlement. Any change in the entitlement requires far greater legislative effort: "A change in a collective limit may provide the basis to amend individual entitlements but this will require the exercise of a Ministerial discretion on a case-by-case basis".[231] West Australia has retained basic structures for the unbundling of water and registering licences. It does not take the water sharing approach that is currently in place in Victoria and New South Wales (as described above) where changes to collective entitlements are more easily spread across all licences. Western Australian licences do not have the same features as their Victorian and New South Wales equivalents where the amount of water actually received depends upon the allocation made to the collective on a seasonal basis.

Western Australia water plans

Plans for water are addressed under Division 3D of the Act. Plans are classified as regional, sub-regional and local area management plans under section 26GV. The Regional Management Plan prepared by the Minister of Water Resources guides the management of water in that region by defining "water resource values, including environmental values as well as the use and integration of water".[232] The preparation of sub-regional plans is also the responsibility of the Minister of Water Resources. Sub-regional plans provide information on "how rights in respect of water are to be allocated to meet various needs, including the needs of the environment", amongst other matters.[233] The hierarchy of plans is based upon their function and the need to follow the regional plan.[234] The public is able to participate in the creation of a plan at the initial stages of plan development. The Department of Water has a crucial role in water allocation planning in Western Australia.

Western Australia is undertaking water law reform with a new Water Resource Management Bill drafted in 2018. The Bill will result in the consolidation of six Acts relating to water into one. The Bill was preceded by the release of a Position Paper on Reforming Water Resource Management in 2013.[235] The reforms covered in the Position Paper included "water allocation planning, licensing, administrative processes, trading, risk assignment and environmental water".[236] The policy drivers for further water law reform included the State's commitments under the National Water Initiative, changes in climate, population growth, expanding economy and other specific issues related to mining.

Summary

This chapter provided an overview of water allocation law and policy in Australia. It focused on the replacement of the riparian doctrine by a statutory system of water allocation as the riparian doctrine became unsuitable for Australian conditions and aspirations for irrigated settlement. The establishment of the Federation and resulting Commonwealth government in 1901 raised tensions over the control and management of water. These tensions were not fully resolved within the Constitution. Over time, clauses relating to trade and external affairs powers were used by the Commonwealth to encourage co-operation in water management.

The example of Victoria provided an account of how regulation assisted in establishing a framework for water markets with environmental water. Water New South Wales and South Australia, the other states in the Murray-Darling Basin, have also unbundled their water entitlements to create water allocations based on a share of water available. They have also created water registers and established legislative frameworks to encourage the development of water markets in meeting the response to the National Water Initiative 2004 and Water Act 2007 (Cth). Western Australia is still undergling the reform process.

Notes

1 Cameron Holley and Darren Sinclair "Rethinking Australian Water Law and Governance: success, Challenges and Future Directions" (2016) 33(4) *EPLJ* 275; Cameron Holley and Darren Sinclair "Governing regulatory markets: Achievements, limitations and the need for reform" (2016) 33(4) *EPLJ* 301; Kate Owens "Reimagining water buybacks in Australia: non-governmental organisations, complimentary initiatives and private capital" (2016) 33(4) *EPLJ* 342; Rebecca Nelson "Broadening regulatory concepts and responses to cumulative impacts: considering the trajectory and future of groundwater law and policy" (2016) 33(4) *EPLJ* 132.

2 Lin Crase "An Introduction to Australian Water Policy" in Lin Crase (ed) *Water Policy in Australia. The Impact of Change and Uncertainty* (Routledge, Washington, 2008) at 4.

3 Paul Kildea and George Williams "The Constitution and the Management of Water in Australia's Rivers" (2010) 32 *Sydney L. Rev.* 595 at 601.

4 Jacqueline Peel and Lee Godden "Australian Environmental Management: A 'Dams' Story" (2005) 28 *University of New South Wales Law Journal* 668 at 670.

5 Kildea and Williams, above n 27, at 601.

6 At 601.

7 At 601.

8 Elizabeth Macpherson, Erin O'Donnell, Lee Godden and Lily O'Neill "Lessons from Australian Water Reforms: indigenous and Environmental Values in Market-based Water Regulation" in Cameron Holley and Darren Sinclair (eds) *Reforming Water Law and Governance* (Springer, Singapore, 2018).

9 *Mabo v Queensland* [No 2] (1992) 175 CLR 1, 36 at 59–60. Confirmed that the legal doctrine of *terra nullius* could not apply where the land was already inhabited. As a result, customary law could apply and indigenous land entitlements remained. In order to prove customary claim to water, a connection with the water as per traditional custom must be proven before a claim is successful.

10 Murray-Darling Basin Authority *A yarn on the river – getting Aboriginal voices into the Basin Plan. Murray-Darling Basin Authority.* (MDBA, Canberra, 2011).

11 National Water Commission *National Water Commission 2009 Biennial Assessment* (NWC, Canberra, 2009). It also commissioned a further report in 2013 NWC *A review of Indigenous Involvement in Water Planning* (National Water Commission, Canberra, 2014).

12 Australian Government *A Module to Support Water Planners and Managers Develop and Implement National Water Initiative Consistent, Inclusive Water Planning and Management Processes that Support Indigenous Social, Spiritual and Customary Objectives* (National Water Commission, Canberra, 2017).

13 Daniel Connell and Quentin Grafton "Water Reform in the Murray Darling Basin" (2011) 47(12) *Water Resour. Res.*

14 Daniel Connell and R. Quentin Grafton. "Water reform in the Murray-Darling Basin" (2011) 47(12) *Water Resour. Res.*

15 For an overview of the history of the Basin and its development see Murray-Darling Basin Authority *Guide to the Proposed Basin Plan* (MDBA, Canberra, 2010).

16 At 13.

17 Australian Bureau of Statistics *4610.0 – Water account, Australia, 2015–16* (ABS, Canberra, 2016); Australian Bureau of Statistics *4618.0 – Water use on Australian farms, 2015–16* (ABS, Canberra, 2017).

18 John Quiggin et al. "Climate change, uncertainty, and adaptation: the case of irrigated agriculture in the Murray-Darling Basin in Australia" (2010) 58(4) *Canadian Journal of Agricultural Economics/Revue* 531; Mac Kirby et al. "Sustainable irrigation: How did irrigated agriculture in Australia's Murray-Darling Basin adapt in the Millennium Drought?" (2014) 145 *Agricultural Water Management* 154; Australian Bureau of Statistics *Gross Value of Irrigated Agricultural Production , 2015–16* (ABS, Canberra, 2017).

19 Daniel Connell and Quentin Grafton "Planning for water security in the Murray-Darling Basin" (2008) 3(1) Public Policy 67 at 6 and Sandford Clark "The River Murray Question: Part II Federation, Agreement and Future Alternatives" (1971) 8 *MULR* 215 at 217.

20 River Murray Waters Act 1915 (Cth).

21 At 598. The agreement was implemented the following year by New South Wales, South Australia and Victoria by passing legislation in 1915.

22 Daniel Connell and Quentin R. Grafton "Water reform in the Murray-Darling Basin" (2011) 47 *Water Resour. Res.* at [10] states "Like all subsequent

intergovernmental agreements, including the most recent reforms in 2007, it excluded land use issues, which remain the preserve of the states".

23 Paul Kildea and George Williams "The Constitution and the Management of Water in Australia's Rivers" (2010) 32 *Sydney L. Rev.* 595–616 at 598.

24 John Williams "Water reform in the Murray-Darling Basin: a challenge in complexity in balancing social, economic and environmental perspectives" (2017) 150(1) J. *Proc. R. Soc. NSW* 68–92.

25 The River Murray Waters Agreement 1915 was amended in 1934 to reflect the use of water for irrigation and the construction of water infrastructure. See River Murray Waters Agreement Amendment Act 1934; John Pigram *Australia's Water Resources: from Use to Management* (CSIRO Publishing, Collingwood, 2007) at 128; Leah M. Gibbs, L.M. "Just add water: colonisation, water governance, and the Australian Inland" (2009) 41 *Environ. Plan. A* 2964–2983; Alexandra Jason. "Evolving governance and contested water reforms in Australia's Murray Darling Basin"(2018) 10(2) *Water* 113.

26 Trevor Langford-Smith and John Rutherford *Water and Land; Two Case Studies in Irrigation* (Australia National University Press, Canberra, 1966) at 3; Bruce Thom "Professor Trevor Langford-Smith, 1916–2011" (2012) 43 *Australian Geographer* 93.

27 Poh-Ling Tan *Legal Issues Relating to Water Use. In Property: Rights and Responsibilities Current Australian Thinking* (Land and Water Australia, Canberra, 2002) at 18.

28 At 18.

29 Examples of state cooperation in dam construction include the 1946 New South Wales and Queensland created the Border Rivers Agreement Snowy Mountains Hydro-Electric Power Act 1949 (Cth). This era was described as "cooperative federalism", particularly in writing that discusses the constitutional issues associated with the passing of Commonwealth Acts affecting state activities for resource development. See James Crawford "The Constitution and the Environment" (1991) 13 *Sydney L. Rev.* 11–30.

30 Tan, above n 27, at 19.

31 At 19.

32 At 20.

33 Daniel Connell and R Quentin Grafton "Planning for water security in the Murray-Darling Basin" (2008) 3(1) *Public Policy* 67 at 68.

34 At 68.

35 Douglas E. Fisher *Australian Environmental Law Norms Principles and Rules* (3rd ed, Lawbook Co, Sydney, 2014).

36 These powers include the overseas and interstate trade power, the trading corporations power, race power and the external affairs power. Refer George Williams, Sean Brennan and Andrew Lynch Blackshield, & Williams Australian *Constitutional Law and Theory Commentary and Materials* (6th ed, The Federation Press, Sydney, 2014).

37 The legal status of the Water Act 2007 (Cth) and the use of constitutional powers was reviewed by the Australian Government Solicitor. See Australian Government Solicitor AGS, *Swimming in New Waters: Recent Reforms to Australian Water Law*, Legal Briefing No. 90, 21 July 2009.

38 Patrick Keyzer *Principles of Australian Constitutional Law 4th* ed (LexisNexis, Chatswood, 2013) at 198.

39 *Convention Concerning the Protection of the World Cultural and Natural Heritage* Treaty Series No. 1037 (1972); and *Convention on Wetlands of*

International Importance especially as Waterfowl Habitat. Ramsar (Iran)
Treaty Series No. 14583 (1971). Jonathan La Nauze and Emma Carmody "Will
the Basin Plan Uphold Australia's Ramsar Convention Obligations?" (2012)
Australian Environment Review 311.

40 Confirmed in *Victoria v Commonwealth* (1996) 187 CLR 416; 138 ALR 129;
70 ALJR 680; BC9603985. Confirmed the precedent in *Commonwealth v
Tasmania* [1983] HCA 21; 158 CLR 1; 57 ALJR 450; 46 ALR 625.

41 Peel and Godden "Australian Environmental Management: A 'Dams' Story',
above n 4, at 672.

42 *Commonwealth v Tasmania* [1983] HCA 21; 158 CLR 1; 57 ALJR 450; 46
ALR 625.

43 Bruce Davis "Adaption and Deregulation in Government Business Enterprise:
The Hydro-Electric Commission of Tasmania 1945–1994" (1995) 54(2) AJPA
252–261 at 254; and Ben Boer "World Heritage Disputes in Australia" (1992)
7 *J. Environ. Law Litig* 248.

44 Pamela F. Walker 1987. *The United Tasmania Group* (Honours dissertation,
University of Tasmania). The world's first green party was formed to lobby
against the dam proposal.

45 Peel and Godden, above n 4, at 672.

46 Barry Cohen, *Minister for Home Affairs and Environment, Parliamentary
Debates* (Parliament of Australia 21 April 1983) at 42 discussing the "World
Heritage Properties Conservation Bill 1983".

47 Adopted by the United Nations Educational, Scientific and Cultural
Organisation (UNESCO) General Conference at its 17th session in Paris on 16
November 1972. *Convention Concerning the Protection of the World Cultural
and Natural Heritage* UNTS. 1037 (1972).

48 Fisher, above n 35, at 109.

49 The earlier case of *Koowarta v Bjelke-Petersen* (1982) 153 CLR 168 had
confirmed that laws passed by the Commonwealth to implement international
treaties must be reasonable and appropriate. See also Keyzer, above n 38,
at 210:

> However, any notion that there was an additional requirement of interna-
> tional concern as suggested by Stephen J in *Koowarta v Bjelke-Petersen*
> (1982) 153 CLR 168 was removed by the Tasmanian Dam case (1983)
> CLR 1.

50 *Richardson v Forestry Commission of Tasmania* (1988) 164 CLR 261;
Queensland v Commonwealth (1989) 167 CLR 232; *Victoria v Commonwealth*
[1996] HCA 56; 187 CLR 416; 138 ALR 129; 66 IR 392 considered in relation to the application of international labour conventions being implemented
at state level; Also cited in *JT International SA v Commonwealth of Australia;
British American Tobacco Australasia Limited v The Commonwealth* [2012]
HCA 43; 250 CLR 1 in relation to the acquisition of property in trademarks.

51 Senate *Legal and Constitutional Affairs References Committee A Balancing
Act: provisions of the Water Act 2007* (Australian Commonwealth Government,
Canberra, 2011) at 19.

52 Wilson Sousa Júnior et al. "Water: drought, crisis and governance in Australia
and Brazil" (2016) 8(11) *Water* 493; Amir Aghakouchak et al. "Australia's
drought: lessons for California" (2014) 343(6718) Science 1430; Mac Kirby
"Sustainable irrigation: how did irrigated agriculture in Australia's Murray-
Darling Basin adapt in the Millennium Drought?" (2014) 145 *Agricultural*

Water Management 154; Anthony S. Kiem "Drought and water policy in Australia: challenges for the future illustrated by the issues associated with water trading and climate change adaptation in the Murray-Darling Basin" (2013) 23(6) *Global Environ. Chang.* 1615; Matt Kendall "Drought and Its Role in Shaping Water Policy in Australia" in Kurt Schwabe et. al. (eds) *Drought in Arid and Semi-arid Regions* (Springer, Dordrecht, 2013) 451.

53 Daniel Connell and Quentin Grafton "Water Reform in the Murray Darling Basin" (2011) 43 *Water Resour. Res.* 1 at 2.

54 Above at 2.

55 Albert van Dijk et al. "The Millennium Drought In Southeast Australia (2001–2009): Natural and Human Causes and Implications for Water Resources, Ecosystems, Economy, and Society" (2013) 49 *Water Resour. Res.* 1040. See also Murray-Darling Basin Authority "Developing the Basin Plan. History of Water Management in the Basin" /www.mdba.gov.au/basin-plan-roll-out/bas in-plan/developing-basin-plan

It took the severe federation drought (1895 to 1902) to bring the states together to start to agree on the management of the Murray. A conference in Corowa in 1902 provided the catalyst, eventually resulting in the River Murray Waters Agreement commencing in 1915 by the governments of NSW, Victoria, South Australia and the Australian Government.

56 L.C. Botterill, D.A. Wilhite (eds), *From Disaster Response to Risk Management: Australia's National Drought Policy* (Springer, Dordrecht, 2005).

57 See Anthony Kiem "Drought and water policy in Australia: challenges for the future illustrated by the issues associated with water trading and climate change adaptation in the Murray-Darling Basin" (2013) 23(6) *Global Environ. Chang.* 1615 for a discussion of the historical drivers of water policy responses to drought.

58 Matthew Heberger "Australia's Millennium Drought: Impacts and Responses" in Peter Gleick (ed) *The World's Water Volume 7. The Biennial Report on Freshwater Resources* (Island Press, Washington, 2012) 97.

59 In 1993, the Council of Australian Governments commissioned a report chaired by Sir Eric Neal to consider water resource issues. Policy Council of Australian Governments. (1994) Sir Eric Neal Report of the Working Group on Water Resource Policy to the Council of Australian Governments.

60 Gerry Bates *Environmental Law in Australia* (5th ed, New South Wales, LexisNexis, 2002) at 73.

61 Crawford, above n 29, at 27.

62 Policy Council of Australian Governments. (1994) Sir Eric Neal Report of the Working Group on Water Resource Policy to the Council of Australian Governments.

63 Above. The Report concerns were summarised in The Council of Australian Governments. Water Reform Framework 1994 at 2.

64 The Council of Australian Government (COAG) *COAG Water Reform Framework 1994 –Attachment A: Water Resource Policy* (Communique, 25 February 1994) at 1: The key objectives of the Council's deliberations were to assist in bringing about a more competitive and integrated national market, and more efficient and effective arrangements for the delivery of services in areas of shared responsibility.

65 Commonwealth of Australia *National Competition Policy Review Report* (the Hilmer Report) August 1993. Following the Inquiry, three intergovernmental

agreements were signed in 1995: the Competition Principles Agreement, the Conduct Code Agreement and the Agreement to Implement the National Competition Policy and Related Reforms.

66 At 5.

67 Productivity Commission *Impact of Competition Policy Reforms on Rural and Regional Australia*, Report No. 8 (Productivity Commission, Canberra, 1999) at 94. Implementation of the NCP programme is split into three tranches. At the end of each tranche – in July of 1997, 1999 and 2001 – the Commonwealth makes the competition grants available to the States and Territories if they are viewed as having made satisfactory progress with the reforms. Assessments are undertaken by the NCC, which monitors each jurisdiction's progress and makes recommendations to the Commonwealth Treasurer. The Commonwealth Government, not the NCC, decides the amount of competition grants actually paid.

68 Objective 4(a) stated a "separation of water property rights from land title and clear specification of entitlements in terms of ownership, volume, reliability, transferability and, if appropriate, quality".

69 National Competition Council *Assessment of government's progress in implementing the National Competition Policy and related reforms 2005* (Commonwealth Government of Australia, Melbourne, 2005) at xvi.

70 Karen Hussey and Steven Dovers "Trajectories in Australian Water Policy" (2006) 135 *Journal of Contemporary Water Resources and Education* 36 at 39.

71 Cameron Holley and Darren Sinclair "Australia's Water Reform Journey – from Stagnation to Innovation" in Cameron Holley and Darren Sinclair (eds) *Reforming Water Law and Governance. From Stagnation to Innovation in Australia* (Springer, Singapore, 2018) at 11. The implementation of the reforms was overseen by the National Competition Council.

72 Thomas Garry "Water Markets and Water Lessons in the United States: Lessons from Australia" (2007) 4(2) *MqJICEL* 23.

73 Rowan Roberts, Nicole Mitchell and Justin Douglas "Water and Australia's Future Economic Growth" (2006) 1 *Economic Round-Up* 53 at 65.

74 K Stoeckel and H. Abrahams (2007) "Water Reform in Australia: the National Water Initiative and the Role of the National Water Commission" in K Hussey and S Dovers (eds) *Managing Water for Australia: the Social and Institutional Challenge* (CSIRO Publishing, Melbourne, 2007).

75 At 65.

76 At 65.

77 The NWI also required water metering requirements in paragraphs 87–89 which required a consistent approach to metering. See Australian Government *National Framework for Non-Urban Water Metering Policy Paper* (Department of Sustainability, Environment, Water, Population and Communities, Canberra, 2009).

78 Lee Godden "Environmental Markets and Property in Water" in Aileen McHarg, Barry Barton, Adrian Bradbrook and Lee Godden (eds) *Property and the Law in Energy and Natural Resources* (Oxford University Press, Oxford, 2010) at 427.

79 Viki Waye and Christina Son "Regulating the Australian Water Market" (2010) 22 J. Environ. Law 431–459 at 437; John Quiggin "Why the Guide to the Proposed Basin Plan Failed, and What Can Be Done to Fix It" in John Quiggin, Thilak Mallawaarachchi and Sarah Chambers (eds) *Water Policy*

Reform, Lessons in Sustainability from the Murray Darling Basin (Edward Elgar, Cheltenham, 2012).

80 The Ministerial Council commissioned an audit of the Basin in 1995. Following the audit, it put in place a temporary cap on water extraction.

81 John Scanlon "A hundred years of negotiations with no end in sight: where is the Murray Darling Basin Initiative leading us?" (2006) 23 *EPLJ* 1 at 6.

82 At 6.

83 Daniel Connell and R Quentin Grafton "Planning for water security in the Murray-Darling Basin" (2008) 3(1) *Public Policy* 67 at 69.

84 Jennifer McKay (2008) "The Legal Frameworks of Australian Water: progression from Common Law Rights to Sustainable Shares" in Lin Crase (ed) *Water Policy in Australia. The Impact of Change and Uncertainty* (RFF Press, Washington, 2008) at 48.

85 Daniel Connell and R Quentin Grafton "Planning for water security in the Murray-Darling Basin" (2008) 3(1) Public Policy 67 at 69. Daniel Connell *Water Politics in the Murray-Darling Basin.* (Federation Press, Sydney 2007).

86 Water Act 2007 (Cth), section 20(b).

87 A Horne, J Freebairn and E O'Donnell "Establishment of environmental water in the Murray Darling Basin: an analysis of two key policy initiatives" (2011) 15(1) *AJWR* 7 at 8.

88 At 8.

89 Benjamin Docker and Ian Robinson "Environmental water management in Australia: experience from the Murray-Darling Basin" (2014) 30 *International Journal of Water Resources Development* 164–177 at 168. This observation was made specifically in relation to America.

90 Department of the Environment Water Heritage and the Arts (DEWHA), *Water for the Future Policy Program* (Canberra, Australian Commonwealth Government, 2010); Operational aspects of the Act are contained in *Intergovernmental Agreement on Murray-Darling Basin Reform 2008* and the 2013 *Intergovernmental Agreement on Implementing Water Reform in the Murray Darling Basin* 2013. The Act incorporates the *Murray Darling Basin Agreement* with reference to it in terms of water sharing and inter-state water transfers in Schedule D of the Act.

91 Cameron Holley and Darren Sinclair "Water Markets and Regulation: implementation, Successes and Limitations" in Cameron Holley and Darren Sinclair (eds) *Reforming Water Law and Governance. From Stagnation to Innovation in Australia* (Springer, Singapore, 2018) 101; Cameron Holley and Darren Sinclair "Compliance and enforcement of water licences in NSW. Limitations in law, policy and institutions". (2012) 15(2) *Australian Journal of Natural Resources Law and Policy* 149.

92 Water Act 2007 (Cth), Part 1 section 3.

93 James Pittock, John Williams and Quentin Grafton. "The Murray-Darling Basin plan fails to deal adequately with climate change". (2015) *Water* 26.

94 Kevin Goss "Environmental flows, river salinity and biodiversity conservation: managing trade-offs in the Murray–Darling Basin" (2003) 51(6) *Australian Journal of Botany* 619.

95 Wentworth Group *Submission to the Senate Inquiry into the urgent provision of water to the Coorong and Lower Lakes* (Wentworth Group, Sydney 2008).

96 Wentworth Group *Sustainable diversions in the Murray-Darling Basin: an analysis of the options for achieving a sustainable diversion limit in the Murray-Darling Basin* (Wentworth Group, Sydney 2010).

97 John Williams "Water reform in the Murray-Darling Basin: a challenge in complexity in balancing social, economic and environmental perspectives" (2017) 150(1) *J. Proc. R. Soc. NSW* 68–92 at 79.

98 The Senate *Parliament of Australia, Rural and Regional Affairs and Transport References Committee: the management of the Murray-Darling Basin, March 2013* (Australian Commonwealth Government, Canberra 2013). http://www.aph.gov.au/Parliamentary_Business/Committees/Senate/Ru ral_and_Regional_Affairs_and_Transport/Completed_inquiries/2012-13/mdb /report/index.

99 James Pittock, John Williams and Quentin Grafton. "The Murray-Darling Basin plan fails to deal adequately with climate change". (2015) Water 26 at 27; Jason Alexandra "Risks, uncertainty and climate confusion in the Murray-Darling Basin reforms" (2017) 3(03) *Water Economics and Policy* 1650038; James Pittock "The Murray-Darling basin: climate change, infrastructure, and water" in Cecilia Tortajada *Increasing Resilience to Climate Variability and Change* (Springer, Singapore, 2016) pp 41–59.

100 Murray-Darling Basin Authority *Sustainable Diversion Limit Adjustment Mechanism: Draft Determination Report* (Australian Government, Canberra, 2017).

101 Bret Walker *Murray Darling Basin Royal Commission* (Government of South Australia, Adelaide, 2019).

102 Murray-Darling Basin Authority "Murray Darling Ministers Meet in Melbourne" *Communique* (14 December 2018).

103 This paragraph draws on the material in "Efficiency Measures – Agreed Criteria" in Murray-Darling Basin Authority "Murray Darling Ministers Meet in Melbourne" *Communique* (14 December 2018).

104 Quentin Grafton and Sarah Wheeler "Economics of water recovery in the Murray-Darling Basin, Australia". (2018) 10 *Annual Review of Resource Economics* 487 at 487.

105 Above.

106 Above.

107 Katherine Owens "Reimagining Water buybacks in Australia: Non-governmental organisations, complementary initiatives and private capital" (2016) 33(4) EPLJ 342 at 343.

108 Above.

109 Grafton and Wheeler (2018), above n 104.

110 At 348.

111 John Williams "Water reform in the Murray-Darling Basin: a challenge in complexity in balancing social, economic and environmental perspectives" (2017) 150(1) *J. Proc. R. Soc. NSW* 68.

112 Information Memorandum *The Murray Darling Basin Balanced Water Fund* (19 October 2015) 3 12.

113 Ben Carr et al. "The Murray-Darling Basin Balanced Water Fund and the Environmental Water Trust–using markets and innovative financing to restore wetlands and floodplains in the Murray-Darling Basin for financial, social and environmental outcomes". Proceedings of the 8th Australian Stream Management Conference, 31 July–3 August 2016. 2016.

114 Erin O'Donnell "Competition or Collaboration? Using Legal Persons to Manage Water for the Environment in Australia and the United States" (2017) 34(6) *EPLJ* 503.

115 Water Act 2007 (Cth), section 93.

116 D.E. Fisher "Water law, the High Court and Techniques of Judicial Reasoning" (2010) 27(2) *EPLJ* at 85.
117 Keyzer above n 38, at 217.
118 Keyzer above n 38, at 218 identified these four points.
119 *ICM Agriculture v The Commonwealth* at 1.
120 At 2.
121 National Water Commission Act 2004 (Cth).
122 *ICM Agriculture v The Commonwealth* at 1.
123 At 8.
124 The Water Rights Act 1896 (NSW) section 1(1) and Water Act 1912 (NSW) section 6 used similar expression.
125 *ICM Agriculture v The Commonwealth* at 10. Specific legislation on bores was also addressed in the Artesian Wells Act 1897 (NSW) and The Water and Drainage and Artesian Wells (Amending) Act 1906 (NSW).
126 Fisher n 70 at 91.
127 *ICM Agriculture v The Commonwealth* 87 at [149] per Hayne, Kiefel and Bell JJ. In paragraphs [142–148], the four points considered in reaching this conclusion are addressed. The first is that water is not like other minerals that can be depleted. The implication of this physical aspect of water is that water control is not just about extraction and use. Water control also includes "ensuring its continuing availability". Secondly, bore licences are "creatures of statute" and none of the licences that were replaced were confirming a prior common law right. Hence, these types of statutory licences were "inherently susceptible to change or termination". Thirdly, it is somewhat misleading and legally incorrect to attach property like terms to groundwater because the groundwater in the aquifer is not ,property in a legal sense until it is controlled by a water user in pipes and so on. In making this point the Court relied upon the precedent in Embery v Owen and Blackstone. The final point was to take into account the State's rights over water. These rights are vested with the State.
128 At [150] per Hayne, Kiefel and Bell JJ.
129 At [84] per French CJ, Gummow and Crennan JJ.
130 Fisher above n 70, at 93.
131 See Janice Gray and Louise Lee "Water Entitlements as Property: a Work in Progress or Watertight Now?" in Cameron Holley and Darren Sinclair (eds) *Reforming Water Law and Governance. From Stagnation to Innovation in Australia* (Springer, Singapore, 2018) 101 for an examination of property theory and whether the National Water Reforms and the existence of water markets are dependent on ascribing property rights to water. The authors question whether it is possible to transfer water entitlements without secure property rights. *Spencer v Commonwealth of Australia* [2015] FCA 754; 240 FCR 282 also followed *ICM Agriculture v The Commonwealth* confirming property rights were not acquired under the Natural Resources Management (Financial Assistance) Act 1992 (Cth) (the NRM Act) and the Natural Heritage Trust of Australia Act 1997 (Cth).
132 Dustin Garrick et al. "Valuing water for sustainable development" (2017) 358 Science1003–1005.
133 Australian Commonwealth Government *Intergovernmental Agreement on a National Water Initiative 2004* (Department of Environment and Energy (Cth), Canberra, 2004).
134 Above at section (81).

135 Above at section 82(2).
136 Above at section 85(i).
137 Above at section 35.
138 Maryanne Slattery, Keryn Chalmers and Jayne M Godfrey "Beyond the Hyrdrographer's Legacy: Water Accounting in Australia" in Jayne M Godfrey and Keryn Chalmers (eds) *Water Accounting International Approaches to Policy Decision-making* (Edward Elgar, Cheltenham, 2012) at 25.
139 At Preamble.
140 Slattery above n 91 at 25–26.
141 Water Accounting Standards Board Water Accounting Conceptual Framework for the Preparation and Presentation of General Purpose Water Accounting Reports (Commonwealth of Australia, Canberra, 2009); Water Accounting Standards Board, Water Accounting Conceptual Framework for the Preparation and Presentation of General Purpose Water Accounting Reports (Commonwealth of Australia, Canberra, 2014).
142 Water Accounting Standards Board, Water Accounting Conceptual Framework for the Preparation and Presentation of General Purpose Water Accounting Reports (Commonwealth of Australia, Canberra, 2014) at 16.
143 Cameron Holley and Darren Sinclair "Governing water markets: Achievements, limitations and the need for regulatory reform" (2016) 33(4) *EPLJ* 301 at 310. In an extensive review of the law and empirical research involving over 4000 participants, Holley and Sinclair provide insight on the achievements of water markets.
144 Above.
145 Cameron Holley and Darren Sinclair, "Compliance and Enforcement of Water Licences in NSW: Limitations in Law, Policy and Institutions" (2012) 15(2) *Australasian Journal of Natural Resources Law and Policy* 149.
146 At 319. This aspect was more prominent for indigenous communities.
147 Lin Crase "An Introduction to Australian Water Policy" in Lin Crase (ed) *Water Policy in Australia. The Impact of Change and Uncertainty* (Routledge, Washington, 2008) at 6.
148 Lee Godden "Environmental Markets and Property in Water" above n 78, at 429.
149 At 309.
150 Water Act 1989 (Vic), section 1.
151 Section 64J.
152 Section 64L(2).
153 Section 64U.
154 Section Sch15(4).
155 Section 33F. A declared water system is as declared by the Minister under section 6A. There are approximately 134 Declared Water Supply Catchments in Victoria. Department of Economic Development, Jobs, Transport and Resources "Declared Water Supply Catchments" http://vro.depi.vic.gov.au/dpi /vro/vrosite.nsf/pages/landuse-water-supply-catchments
156 Water Act 1989 (Vic), section 33F(2). Provides specific guidance regarding shares owned by more than one person.
157 Water Act 1989 (Vic), section 33F(2)(a) and section 33F(2)(b).
158 Water Act 1989 (Vic), section 33S(2).
159 See discussion by Lee Godden "Environmental Markets and Property in Water", above n 78, at 413.

160 Water Act 1989 (Vic), section 34(1) also makes provision for those holding licences under the Water Industry Act 1994, the Electricity Act 2000 and the Conservation, Forests and Lands Act 1987.

161 Formerly referred to as the Minister for Water.

162 Water Act 1989 (Vic), section 40 (l) and section 40 (m).

163 Water Act 1989 (Vic), section 40(o).

164 Water Act 1989 (Vic), section 43(a).

165 Water Act 1989 (Vic), section 43(c).

166 Above, section 43 (d) and section 43(e).

167 Above, section 84B.

168 Above, section 84B.

169 Above, section 84C(2).

170 Victorian Water Register, "Trading Rules" Available at http://waterregister.vic. gov.au/water-trading/trading-rules

171 Water Act 1989 (Vic), section 84C.

172 Water Act 1989 (Vic), Part 4, Division 1A.

173 Water Act 1989 (Vic), section 48C.

174 This paragraph and the discussion on the Victorian Environmental Water Holder draws extensively on the work of Erin O'Donnell "Institutional Reform in Environmental Water Management: The New Victorian Environmental Water Holder" (2011) 22 *Journal of Water Law* 73 at 76 and Erin O'Donnell and Elizabeth MacPherson "Challenges and Opportunities for Environmental Water Management in Chile: An Australian Perspective" (2011) 23 *Water Law* 24.

175 O'Donnell (2011) above at 76.

176 At 77.

177 Water Act 1989 (Vic), section 33AAA.

178 Water Act 1989 (Vic), section 33.

179 O'Donnell (2011) above n 126, at 80.

180 At 80 citing Rachel Kleinman "Dead fish fear for the Yarra" The Age (13 November 2007).

181 At 80.

182 Environmental Defenders Office "Reforming the Environmental Water Reserve: How amendments to Victoria's Water Act could restore river health" (Environmental Defenders Office, Melbourne, 2010).

183 At 4.

184 At 4.

185 Above. The "White Paper" is Department of Sustainability and the Environment, Securing Our Water Future Together: Victorian Government White Paper (2004).

186 Water Act 1989 (Vic), section 33DB(2)(a) and section 33DB(2)(c).

187 Section 33DF(2).

188 Section 33DH(2).

189 Section 33DY.

190 Section 33DY(2)(b).

191 Section 33DY(4).

192 Victorian Environmental Water Holder *Water Allocation Trading Strategy 2018–2019.* (VEWH, Melbourne, 2018) has indicated that it can sell water to northern regions if environmental water needs are met.

193 Victorian Environmental Water Holder "VEWH water sale in northern Victoria – March 2015" (2015) Available at www.vewh.vic.gov.au/news-and-resources/ news/vewh-water-sale-in-northern-victoria-march-2015

194 Warwick Long "Liberal MP wants Murray-Darling water sold to irrigators so government authority can pay its way" *ABC Rural* (27 April 2015).

195 Above.

196 Debroah Curran and Sharon Mascher "Adaptive Management in Water Law: Evaluating Australian (New South Wales) and Canadian (British Columbia) Law Reform Initiatives" (2016) 12(1) *McGill International Journal of Sustainable Development Law* at 91.

197 Lin Crase, Leo O'Reilly and Brian Dollery "Water markets as a vehicle for water reform: the case of New South Wales" *Aust. J. Agric. Resour. Econ.* 44(2) 299 at 300.

198 H.N Turral and others "Water trading at the margin: the evolution of water markets in the Murray Darling Basin" *Water Resour. Res.* 41 (2005) 1 at 1.

199 National Competition Council "Assessment of government's progress in implementing the National Competition Policy and related reforms 2005" (Commonwealth Government of Australia, Melbourne, 2005) at xxi.

200 At 2.

201 Irrigation Corporations Act 1994 (NSW). Division 3 makes reference to any debts owing to the state and where the funds will be deposited.

202 Water Management Act 2000 (NSW), section 116.

203 Paul Taylor, Tony McGlynn and Warren Martin "The influence of privatisation on irrigation water rights in NSW" Paper for presentation at the Regional Conference of the International Association for the Study of Common Property, Brisbane, Australia, September 2001 at 10–11.

204 See also Irrigation Corporations Act 1994, section 53.

205 It progressively replaced the Water Act 1912 (NSW).

206 Water Management Act 2000 (NSW), section 393.

207 The Water Management Act 2000 (NSW), section 6(3)(a) contained the requirement to give effect to "government obligations arising under any inter-governmental agreement to which the government is a party, such as the Murray-Darling Basin Agreement set out in Schedule 1 to the Water Act 2007 of the Commonwealth". The Act is administered by the New South Wales Office of Water.

208 Water Management Act 2000 (NSW), section 58(1)(a).

209 Water Management Act 2000 (NSW), sections 69 and 70.

210 NSW Department of Primary Industries Water "Delivering Water Resource Plans for New South Wales Roadmap 2016–2019. (November 2016).

211 Murray-Darling Basin Authority *Water Resource Plan – December 2018 Quarterly Report* (Australian Government, Canberra, 2018) at 7.

212 Australian Broadcasting Corporation *Four Corners Program – Pumped* (Monday 24 July 2017).

213 New South Wales Department of Industry *Response to ABC 4 Corners Inquiry* (20 July 2017).

214 Bret Walker *Murray Darling Basin Royal Commission* (Government of South Australia, Adelaide, 2019).

215 Anne Davis "Hundreds of thousands of native fish dead in second Murray-Darling incident" *The Guardian* (7 January 2019).

216 Natural Resources Act 2004 (SA), section 45.

217 Natural Resources Act 2004 (SA), section 44(1).

218 Barbara Cosens "Governing the Freshwater Commons: Lessons from Application of the Trilogy of Governance Tools in Australia and the Western United States" in Cameron Holley and Darren Sinclair (2018) *Reforming Water*

Law and Governance. From Stagnation to Innovation in Australia (Springer, Singapore, 2018) at 288.

219 Natural Resources Management Act 2004 (SA) section 48(2)(a).

220 Natural Resources Management Act 2004 (SA), section 48(2)(b).

221 Rowan Roberts, Nicole Mitchell and Justin Douglas "Water and Australia's Future Economic Growth" (2006) 1 *Economic Round-Up* 53.

222 Natural Resources Management Act 2004 (SA), section 146(1).

223 Natural Resources Management Act 2004 (SA), section 124(4).

224 Irrigation Act 2009 (SA), section 32(1)(c).

225 Natural Resources Management Act 2004 (SA), section 74.

226 Government of South Australia Our Place. Our Future. State Natural Resources Management Plan South Australia 2012–2017 (Government of South Australia, Adelaide, 2012) at 3.

227 Natural Resources Management Act 2004 (SA), section 75.

228 National Competition Council "Assessment of government's progress in implementing the National Competition Policy and related reforms 2005" (Commonwealth Government of Australia, Melbourne, 2005) at xxxi. Ten percent of its payments from the Council were suspended and the matter deemed to be more appropriate for the National Water Commission.

229 Rights in Water and Irrigation Amendment Act 2000 (WA).

230 Michael Bennett "Adjusting Collective Limits on the Use of Natural Resources: Approaches in Australian Fisheries and Water Law" (2015) 34(1) *UTLR* 68.

231 At 68.

232 Rights in Water and Irrigation Amendment Act 2007 (WA), section 26GW(2).

233 Rights in Water and Irrigation Amendment Act 2007 (WA), section 26GX(2b).

234 Government of Western Australia *Water Allocation Planning in Western Australia A Brief Overview* (Department of Water, Perth, 2011).

235 Department of Water (2013) *Securing Western Australia's Water Future. Position Paper – Reforming Water Resource Management* (Government of Western Australia, Perth, 2013).

236 At 1.

5 Comparative analysis

Introduction

This chapter examines the lessons that New Zealand can learn from Australia's experience in water law and policy development. Whereas New Zealand has not embarked upon extensive water allocation law reform, Australia does provide a valuable example of significant water allocation law reform. The comparative analysis in this chapter focuses on answering the research question by addressing the problems identified during New Zealand's water policy gap from 1991 until 2011. These problems related to the lack of alternatives to the "first in, first served" method of water allocation, the lack of opportunities to transfer water between users without heavy administration, addressing how to develop cohesive national guidance on water allocation law and policy development and generally how to achieve good water allocation for all water users.

It begins by examining the legal authority of national institutions responsible for the development of water law and policy. In Australia, this role has been fulfilled by the National Water Commission. The responsibility for New Zealand water policy development is split across government departments, including the Ministry for the Environment and Ministry for Primary Industries (responsible for water for irrigation). New Zealand is facing problems following a lack of national water policy from 1991 until 2011. It is worth addressing whether a national authority would assist in implementing water allocation law reform.

The "first in, first served" method of water allocation has been a problem for New Zealand. It has contributed to the problem of fully allocated catchments with limited means to facilitate transfer between water users. One of the underlying issues affecting water transfers is that New Zealand water allocations are tied to the land. If water permits were separated (unbundled) from the land, it would assist in developing other water products to improve water transfers. The Australian experience shows that after unbundling, there are greater chances to develop new water products. Unbundling would assist New Zealand in addressing the question of how to find alternative methods to allocate water, other than the "first in, first served" method. As we have seen, the "first in, first served" method of water allocation creates a "gold rush" effect in catchments that are close to full allocation. Water demand increases as potential users rush to ensure they have made an application for water they may require. Demand for water in catchments needs to be addressed to assist with water transfers. Australia provides various examples of water products in the form of unbundled water shares, water delivery rights and so on. Australian states provide legal rights to irrigators that New Zealand irrigators do not have. Regulation of rights for irrigators in light of the Australian experience deserves further attention.

The "first in, first served" method of water allocation does not allow the comparison of one application against another. The different volume of two takes cannot be considered when determining the outcome of each water permit application. There is no statutory distinction in New Zealand for large water takes that are for municipal supply, irrigation or electricity generation. Yet, these categories of water take involve significant investment in infrastructure to manage the water allocation. Australian states generally classify such water takes as "bulk water" applications and the regulatory process for determining whether they are granted or not can take into account infrastructure investment and state interests. It is worthwhile to consider the potential benefits of legal recognition of bulk water applications in New Zealand.

Embarking upon changes to unbundle should be complemented with an increased systematic collection of information on water takes. In the Australian experience, this information is not just for water users but also other stakeholders such as the public, government and financial institutions. Furthermore, the information is not just hydrometric. It also includes adjustments for seasonal or temporary takes, security interests, owners, the nature of the water permit and the level of security ascribed to the water permit. In response to the need to benchmark and report this water allocation related information, Australia developed water accounting standards. The standards assist in communicating water information with a broader range of users. This analysis considers to what extent a similar approach to the collection and dissemination of water information would be useful in New Zealand.

The last point of comparison in this chapter examines the role of environmental water. Australia has taken a novel approach in establishing an Environmental Water Holder at the Commonwealth and state level (dependent on state implementation). However, New Zealand does not have a comparable office.

In terms of water scarcity, Australia is certainly in a different position from New Zealand. Australia has been required to respond decisively to evidence of physical water scarcity, particularly in the Murray-Darling Basin. The Australian response to water scarcity was implementing water markets as part of a cap and trade system (not a free market), which is heavily regulated.[1] It was seen as an innovator in developing water allocation law and policy. More recently, the Australian progress in water law reform implementation has stagnated.[2] There are also concerns about the effectiveness of regulation and enforcement of the cap on water abstraction.[3] Regardless of these concerns, Australia has undertaken significant steps to address water allocation issues.

In comparison to Australia, New Zealand is experiencing economic water scarcity, not physical water scarcity such as with the effect of the Millennium Drought. Evidence of economic water scarcity in New Zealand includes some regional catchments which have become fully allocated or over-allocated, such as in the Canterbury region. New Zealand can learn from the Australian experience of undertaking extensive water law reform to improve water allocation outcomes. The Australian experience in implementing water allocation law has been complex and challenging. New Zealand can learn from both the success and shortcomings of Australian water law reform.

Comparative analysis table

Table 5.1 compares the key features of Australian states' water allocation law and policy with New Zealand. It compares New Zealand with the Australian states of Victoria, New South Wales, South Australia and Western Australia. This comparison provides an account of how water allocation law and policy of individual states differ from New Zealand. The comparison table draws upon the case studies provided in the previous chapter (Table 5.1).

The Resource Management Act (RMA) is the primary legislation addressing water allocation in New Zealand. It included a provision for resource management plans and policies to be prepared at the national and regional level.[4] The review of water allocation law and policy in New Zealand since the enactment of the RMA established that the full implementation of the RMA for water allocation would be complete only once the plans at the national and regional level were prepared. However, in contrast to the Australian situation, it was not compulsory to prepare these plans under the RMA, but it was one of the "functions" of councils under the RMA.[5] While most regional plans were prepared, they were weak in their effectiveness in terms of managing water allocation or preventing over-allocation. Furthermore, no national

Table 5.1 Key features of Australian states water allocation law and policy with New Zealand

	New Zealand	Victoria	New South Wales	South Australia	Western Australia
State Legislation					
Main Water Allocation Legislation	Resource Management Act 1991 (NZ)	Water Act 1989 (Vic)	Water Management Act 2000 (NSW)	Natural Resources Management Act 2004 (SA)	Rights in Water and Irrigation Act 1914 (WA)
Is there a commitment to sustainability in the objects of the Act?	Yes Section 5.	Yes Section 1(d)	Yes Section 3".	Yes Section 7(1)	Yes Section 4
Is there a separate Act for water management?	No	Yes	Yes	No	Yes
Does the Act also include provisions relating to water for irrigation?	No The Irrigation Schemes Act 1990 privatised Irrigation Schemes.	Yes Part 11 of the Act covers Irrigation which applies to an "Authority" that includes an "Irrigation District".	Yes Part 1 of the Act covers all Irrigation Corporations formed under the Irrigation Corporations Act 1994 (section 116). Part 2 covers private irrigation districts	No Irrigation Act 2009 (SA) Rights under the Act may be converted to a water licence under the Natural Resources Management Act 2004 (SA) under section 32(1)(c) of the Irrigation Act 2009 (SA).	Yes Part IV Irrigation Districts
Water Register					
Is there a National/state water register?	No Water Permit information is held by regional councils. Securities against water permits may be registered on the Personal Property Securities Register.	Yes Section 84B	Yes Water Access Licence Register (section 71)	Yes Schedule 3A	Yes Division 3E
Is it a public register	Information can be requested regarding water permits. Yes, the securities register is a public register.	Yes	Yes	Yes	Yes
Does the water register record security interests?	NA New Zealand does not have a water register	Yes Mortgage interests on water shares in Schedule 12A	Yes Recorded on security interest with evidence in approved form (section 71D)	Yes Natural Resources Management Act 2004 (SA) Schedule 3A	Yes Division 3E Register of Instruments 26GZM

Does the water register require notice to third parties to change the security interest?	The PPSR does not require notice to the third party of changes.		Yes Notifications for changes to mortgage interests on security shares in Schedule 12A	Yes Schedule 3A regulates the creation, priority, variation, transfer, discharge and enforcement of a security interest.	Yes Division 3E Register of Instruments 26GZO Holder of the security interest to be notified of certain events
Are there statutory provisions relating to the type of information that must be provided?	Not specifically about water permits, i.e. the volume of water allocated. Water permits may be registered as "goods" on the Personal Property Securities Register under section 122(4) of the RMA.		Yes Division 1 Section 84A–84E	Yes Schedule 1A	Yes Division 3E

Water Allocation — Statutory Categories

"Water Allocation" Terminology	A water allocation is the event or process of making an allocation of water under a water permit.	Water allocation means the volume of water granted once an application for water has been determined Section 3 of the Water Act 1989 (Vic) defines "water allocation" by categorising it into environmental entitlement, bulk water and water licence. The final water allocation for environmental water and bulk water is based on a seasonal determination or under the terms of the entitlement if there is no seasonal determination made. The final allocation for water shares is the volume allocated to the particular share at any time.	Water allocation means the volume of water granted once an application for water has been determined under the water access licence There are three broad categories of licences: domestic use and town water supply, high security licences and general security licences. Actual water allocation is based on annual declarations and a system of water management plans.	Water allocation means the volume of water granted once an application for water has been determined under a water licence as defined in section 3 of the Natural Resources Management Act 2004 (SA)	Water allocation means the volume of water granted once an application for water has been determined. Under The Rights in Water and Irrigation Act 1914 (WA), "water entitlement" as defined in sections 26Q(3), Sch. 1 cl. 17(4), Sch. 1 cl. 28 and Sch. 1 cl. 37.

Water Allocation - Bulk Water

Bulk water is a category of water allocation	No statutory distinction between applications for high volumes of water and smaller takes	Yes section 34(1)(a) for "water supply or irrigation"	Yes Major Utility category of Water Access Licence section 57(i)	Yes Categories of water licence exist for some categories of bulk water take such as municipal water supply and irrigation schemes.	No statutory distinction within the Act for all bulk water; however, there are separate processes for irrigation water and water supply

(Continued)

Table 5.1 Continued

	New Zealand	Victoria	New South Wales	South Australia	Western Australia
Bulk water allocations processing and priority	Regional councils follow administrative procedures in the RMA. There is priority for all applications by order of time or "first come, first served" principle as per the precedent in *Fleetwing Farms v Marlborough District Council.*	Decided separately from other water use applications at the Department level	Water supplier licences are given priority over all other categories of water access licences section 58.	Subject to provisions in Natural Resource Management Plans	Not applicable
Principles of water allocation	No distinction for any water permit application based on volume, including bulk water. Applications are decided at the regional council following the "first come, first served" rule to assess the merits of the application without making comparisons with existing or future applications	Section 40 gives the Minister broad discretion. Under section 40(1) the Minister "must have regard to" any Ministerial report prepared under the Act, existing and projected water availability, avoiding adverse effects on the environment, any existing water allocations made to the applicant, Government policies on water allocation and conservation, the purpose for which the water is to be used and the needs of other potential applicants	Rules for bulk water applications are included under section 20 of the Act as part of water management plans that must be prepared for each area. The rules must be in accordance with priorities under section 58 for water access licences.	Regional Water Allocation Plans are prepared following the provisions of the Act. Once the Plans are prepared they must also be accredited. The Plans include limits on water allocations. The water allocation plan will state where applications for new takes are restricted and if so it will outline how new allocations can be acquired through trading.	Does not have separate provisions for bulk water as part of the comprehensive water allocation legislation. Water allocations in regional plans cap consumptive use for particular categories of water take such as irrigation or hydropower. These limits are contained at the regional level once plans are developed. Further water law reform may be able to address this area in a more comprehensive manner.
Water Allocation – Environmental Water Is environmental water legally recognised as a separate legal entity for the purposes of water allocation?	Not for the purposes of holding water allocations or water rights. There is legal recognition of the Wanganui River as part of the settlement process with local Maori tribes that does not affect existing water allocations.	Yes	Yes	Yes	Yes

Water Allocation – Unbundling (Water allocation in entitlements, licences and shares)

Can the environmental water holder participate in the water market?	N/A	Yes. The Commonwealth Environmental Water Holder can buy water for the environment. State environmental water holders, such as the Victorian Environmental Water Holder, can also participate in the market to ensure that water is returned to the environment. Market participation and water buy-back schemes by the government have been a contentious part of the reform process. Some rural communities in particular feel that they are unfairly bearing the burden of the effect of the reforms as it returns water to the environment by purchasing it from existing water holders who might otherwise operate businesses in the area.			
Principles for water allocation	N/A	Broad Ministerial Discretion to make environmental water allocations under section 48F. The Minister can consider potential adverse effects on existing users, government policies on conservation and water allocation, water management plans and any other matters the Minster thinks fit.	Office of Environment and Heritage holds environmental water. It is ensuring that the water holdings are in accordance with the requirements of the Water Act 2007(Cth) which requires the plans to be accredited. New South Wales has experienced some issues with meeting the requirements of the Water Act 2007(Cth) on time.	Environmental water allocations are a part of the natural resource management planning process. Environmental water is held by the Murray Darling Basin Authority, Commonwealth Environmental Water Holder and the South Australian government.	Subject to current reform as there is limited reference to environmental water planning under the Act. Environmental water planning is subject to Ministerial discretion.
Are water allocations tied to land (bundled)?	Statutory scheme of water allocation which distinguishes between water take and use. In practice, water take and use are still often 'bundled' together. Actual water allocation is a fixed entitlement recorded on the water permit, unless the regional plan allows for a class of water that has lower reliability.	No	No	No	No
Water allocation		Unbundled and actual water allocation will vary according to share available or declared. • Water use licence (sections 64J, 64L) • Delivery licence(Sch15)4) • Water Share (sections 33F) • Bulk Entitlements (section 34(1)(a) for 'water supply or irrigation' (Bulk Entitlement Allocations are discussed in this table).	Unbundled and actual water allocation will vary according to share available or declared. Water Access Licence with a 'share component' which is expressed as maximum volume, proportion of available water, proportion of storage capacity of a dam or a specific number of units.	Unbundled and actual water allocation will vary according to share available or declared • Forest water licence section 169(c) • Well drillers licence section139 • Water access entitlement Chapter 7, Part 3	Unbundled Actual water allocation is still a fixed entitlement but can be traded in full or part separately from the land.
Nature of statutory property rights in a water permit (NZ) /unbundled allocation	Section 122(1) of the RMA states that 'A resource consent is neither real nor personal property.'	Can deal with the unbundled water licence or water allocation as personal property.	Can deal with the unbundled water licence or water allocation as personal property.	Can deal with the unbundled water licence or water allocation as personal property.	Can deal with the unbundled water licence or water allocation as personal property.

(Continued)

Table 5.1 Continued

	New Zealand	Victoria	New South Wales	South Australia	Western Australia
Court's Interpretation of Property Rights in a Water Permit (NZ) / Unbundled Allocation	Contention regarding the application of property law concepts to resolving water permit issues. The nature of rights in a water permit in common law does recognise elements of property for the holder of the consent.	*ICM Agriculture v The Commonwealth* confirmed that property rights were not gained by the Commonwealth when the irrigator's entitlements under new legalisation were reduced.			
Principles for water allocation		For the Water Use Licence, the relevant principles are in section 64U, which are focused on limiting the adverse effects of irrigation at the location of the water take. The adverse effects include reducing the effects of salinity, managing groundwater infiltration, protecting biodiversity and reducing the cumulative effects of water use. Water Shares-Broad Ministerial Discretion under section 33J. First under section 33J(1), where there is a bulk entitlement in the zone or a "permissible consumptive volume has been declared" the Minister must ensure that the issue of a water share is "consistent" with the pre-existing bulk entitlement and it is "not likely to have" an effect on other water shares, environmental entitlements and "the needs of other potential applicants".	Water access licences are issued based on being in accordance with relevant water management plans and not have an adverse effect on the environment. Water access licences are given priority under the Act. First priority is given to domestic water and town water supply, second priority is given to high security licences and third priority is given to general licences. Once the water available is declared then the water access licence holder will know what percentage of their licence they have been allocated. Hence priorities between different water allocations is based on the type of licence held.	Regional Water Allocation Plans are prepared following the provisions of the Act. Once the Plans are prepared they must also be accredited. The Plans include limits on water allocations. The water allocation plan will state where applications for new takes are restricted and if so it will outline how new allocations can be acquired through trading.	The principles for granting a water licence are contained in Schedule 1 section 7 of the Act. The Minister has broad discretion to refuse a licence application. The Minister must have regard whether the application is "in the public interest", "ecologically sustainable", "environmentally acceptable", could affect current or future water needs, would be detrimental to others in the Minister's opinion, could have another source of water, keeps within local practices and bylaws, or is consistent with planning instruments.

The second category is where section 33J(1) does not apply. Under section 33J(2)(a) to (k) the requirements are that the Minister "must consider" the "existing and projected" availability and quality of water, potential "adverse effect" on existing uses of water, waterways, aquifers and the environmental water reserve, other water shares already owned by the applicant, "the need to protect the environment" and government conservation policy, any adverse effect there could be on maintaining the environmental water reserve, "the needs of other potential applicants" and relevant report or inquires under any Act

- Other matters that the Minister "thinks fit to have regard to".

National Water Initiative 2004
Water Act 2007 (Cth) and the Murray-Darling Basin Plan
National Competition Reforms to promote improved efficiency in water management

National Water Initiative 2004
Water Act 2007 (Cth) and the Murray-Darling Basin Plan
National Competition Reforms to promote improved efficiency in water management

National Water Initiative 2004
Water Act 2007 (Cth) and the Murray-Darling Basin Plan
National Competition Reforms to promote improved efficiency in water management

National Water Initiative 2004
Water Act 2007 (Cth) and the Murray-Darling Basin Plan
National Competition Reforms to promote improved efficiency in water management

Water Allocation Plans
National

Gap in national planning and policy from 1991 to 2011. National Policy Statement for Freshwater Management 2014 (Amended in 2017)

(Continued)

Table 5.1 Continued

	New Zealand	Victoria	New South Wales	South Australia	Western Australia
Australian States and New Zealand Regions	Regional policy statements and plans to be prepared by regional councils. However, not all Councils prepared Water Allocation Plans.	Sustainable Water Strategies established from 2006 to 2011.*	State Water Management Outcomes Plan which has a lifespan of 5 years. Strong direction in the Water Management Act 2000 (NSW) objects. Also regional water plans that state limits applicable to water access licences.	State Natural Resources Management Plan is required under the Natural Resources Act 2004 (SA). Also Regional Natural Resources Management Plans prepared by the Natural Resources Management Board.	Plans are required under the Rights in Water and Irrigation Act 1914. Regional, sub-regional and local plans for water management prepared by the Department of Water. Subject to further reform as Plans are not compulsory to prepare
Recording and Reporting Water Data					
National water statistics	Until recently the Department of Statistics and Ministry for the Environment prepared separate reports on water data. A joint report is now prepared.	Reported to and collated by the Bureau of Meteorology under the Water Act 2007 (Cth).	Reported to and collated by the Bureau of Meteorology under the Water Act 2007 (Cth).	Reported to and collated by the Bureau of Meteorology under the Water Act 2007 (Cth).	Reported to and collated by the Bureau of Meteorology under the Water Act 2007 (Cth).
Regional reporting of water information is standardised	Regional councils may develop their independent methods for collecting, storing and reporting data. Scientifically based as hydrological data. Regional reports carried out by regional councils or their consultants	Yes. Through the use of Water Accounting Standards	Yes. Through the use of Water Accounting Standards	Yes. Through the use of Water Accounting Standards	Yes. Through the use of Water Accounting Standards

Business reporting and use of water information including financial institutions	No	Yes	Yes	Yes	Yes
	Water information relates to hydrological characteristics. The Australian Water Accounting Standards have not been adopted in New Zealand. New Zealand government has established Guidelines for Councils to Report Water.	Through the use of Water Accounting Standards	Through the use of Water Accounting Standards	Through the use of Water Accounting Standards	Through the use of Water Accounting Standards

Source: Compiled by the author from the analysis of sources referred to in the preceding chapters, including relevant water law.

* Victoria State Government, Department of Environment, Land, Water and Planning "Sustainable Water Strategies" www.water.vic.gov.au/planning-and-entitlements/water-resource-planning/sustainable-water-strategies

policy instrument was prepared for water allocation from 1991 to 2011, a state of affairs that resulted in a policy gap. Chapter 3 critically evaluated the policy gap and its implications. During the national policy gap, water allocation was carried out on a regional level through rules in regional plans. Essentially, between 1991 and 2011, water allocation plans and policy development occurred without national guidance.[6]

As has been stated earlier in the book, under the RMA New Zealand does not have a national water commission. Previously, New Zealand did have a national body responsible for water allocation policy development, a body which was established under the Water and Soil Conservation Act 1967. That body – the New Zealand National Water and Soil Conservation Authority – had a comparable role to the Australian National Water Commission. The Act defined the statutory role of the National Water and Soil Conservation Authority, reflecting its extensive powers. The Authority was meant to collect information on existing and future water allocation. It was able to inquire into "future requirements" for water allocation and "competing demands".[7] When making decisions on water allocation, it had to consider the "best use" of water.[8] In 1988, the Authority was abolished, and its powers were placed with those of regional water boards.[9] National oversight of water policy development and many of the functions of the Authority were devolved to the regional level.

Lessons from Australia on the role of national water institutions

As has been shown, the Australian Commonwealth government overcame significant constitutional barriers when implementing water law reform.[10] The examination of the Australian Constitution in Chapter 6 showed that the Commonwealth Government did not have express constitutional powers to allocate water.[11] Instead, it relied upon a variety of other constitutional powers to encourage states to co-operate on changes to water law and policy. Because of the constitutional context, it was important for the Commonwealth to work with the momentum of state agreement and to move relatively quickly to implement changes across states.[12] The National Water Initiative 2004 and the Water Act 2007 (Cth) ensured that all states worked towards a common goal of implementing water law reform.[13] The National Water Initiative 2004 provided the blueprint for state water law reform and the implementation of water markets.[14] The National Water Commission was also established to provide continued support and leadership for water law reform implementation. It is therefore important to evaluate the reasons for the establishment and abolition of the Commission, notably to explore whether the Commission was abolished because it had fulfilled its statutory objective or whether other reasons contributed to its demise.

The Australian experience shows that it is essential to understand the role of national institutions in implementing water allocation reform. The National Water Commission provided an independent voice that gave much-needed transparency to the water reform process in Australia. There are therefore several reasons why New Zealand should establish a National Water Commission to implement comprehensive water reform like Australia. Water allocation law reform will take a long time and having the independent oversight of a National Water Commission will assist in systematically implementing the reforms while also providing support to the various stakeholders affected. The Commission should be a permanent body with similar responsibilities to those which Australia's National Water Commission had to report on future water demand.

Much of the New Zealand economy depends on water to produce commodities. Currently, the Ministry for the Environment does not have responsibility for water for agricultural production. As stated earlier, irrigation water policy development is the responsibility of the Ministry for Primary Industries. As demand grows for water because of climate change, population growth and economic growth, decisions about water allocation will only become more difficult. A central independent body would be the best means to bring the same transparency to water allocation policy development in New Zealand as the National Water Commission has done in Australia. The current quasi-judicial regionalised approach to water allocation decision making is not a long-term solution for New Zealand. There are examples of high-profile water allocation applications being decided by councils following the "first come, first served" rule, which have broader implications for the New Zealand environment and economy.[15] The critical evaluation in Chapter 5 explained the problems facing New Zealand water allocation as stated in the Land and Water Forum Reports. The Reports are comprehensive in terms of identifying the barriers that water permit holders face when wanting to transfer water permits. While high profile media coverage is provided to water bottling exports, the impact of water bottling may not be at the same scale as water takes for other uses, such as irrigation. That is not to say that water permits for water bottling should remain unregulated. Rather, the argument is that a wider and more comprehensive view of water allocation issues in New Zealand should be examined for their long-term impact.

A New Zealand water register

New Zealand does not have a water register. One of the functions of councils is to hold information relating to water permits; however, that function does not include recording information about security interests attached to water permits.[16] In New Zealand, the registration of security interests relating to water permits is maintained under the Personal Property Security Act 1999. The Comparative Analysis Table shows gaps in the use of a water register for the registration and removal of securities. For example, in New Zealand it is not compulsory to register the security interest over a water permit. In Victoria, New South Wales, South Australia and Western Australia, the registration of security interests over water licences are required in order to provide information to third parties. As stated in the Comparative Analysis Table, all these states provide for comprehensive details regarding the type of information that must be required. In New Zealand, the information regarding water permits is currently split between councils and the Personal Property Securities Register. The establishment of a water register would, therefore, assist in providing a transparent public record of water permits in one place. The ease of access to information relating to water allocation is evident in the Australian experience. In Australia, there is a wide range of people who seek access to water allocation information for a range of purposes, from irrigators verifying the volume of water allocated to them to banks using water allocations as collateral for loans.

Currently, in New Zealand purchasers of a business using water permits may rely upon record keeping by regional councils to verify consent conditions, a reliance which could raise significant legal issues.[17] The reality is that water permits are a valuable part of business transactions.[18] The recording of water permits in a national water register will standardise the collection of water permit information and the registration of security interests. Section 122(4) of the RMA already allows for the recognition of resource consents, including water permits, as "goods" to be registered on the Personal Property Security Register.

In the process of unbundling, the state of Victoria considered the link between information in the land register and the need to verify land and water information:[19]

> As part of the conversion process accurate land ownership data is required, particularly to ensure accuracy of the mortgage is maintained. This requires a comparison of some of the information in the water authority records and the land registry records, and to enable this to occur the legislation specifically authorises the use of the information in those records for cross-checking.

The point raised in the quote above is a very practical one. It recognises that land and water were bundled together as assets that could then be used to provide security for mortgages or other loans. The process of unbundling water permits required regulation to maintain the legal obligations in existing mortgages and other securities. As shown in the Comparative Analysis

Table, all the Australian states analysed have established a water register. The water register provides the legal definition of rights regarding the name of the owner, quantity, location of the take, the price of transfer and location, and the registration of security interests. The Comparative Analysis Table also shows that notice must be given to third parties with a registered security interest if certain events occur.

In comparison, in New Zealand, the registration of security interests attached to water permits does not require third party notification. A benefit of a separate water register would be that it enables changes to the underlying security to trigger the notification to a registered third party. The economic value of a water permit would be protected by the creation of a water register in New Zealand. New Zealand needs the requisite protection for the transfer of water permits to higher-value use by providing the appropriate level of protection to businesses that rely on the value of their water allocation for lending purposes.

New Zealand should consider the consolidation of water permit information in the form of a water register that is similar to Australia's register. A New Zealand water register would improve the reliability of water permit information by recording it in a public register. Furthermore, it would recognise the economic value of water as an asset of businesses relying upon water allocation to operate successfully.

Recording and reporting of water data

As described in the previous chapter, policy objectives in the COAG Framework 1994 required the development of water information collection. The comprehensive nature of the Australian reforms meant that this included the development of water accounting standards. The collection of water information and data is a key part of measuring the success of the Commonwealth-led water law reform. In Australia, water accounting was included in the water reform process on the basis that "high quality information is necessary to base sound decisions relating to water management".[20] Before the reforms, water accounts were kept mainly for internal technical purposes and users. The shift towards broader general purpose water resource accounting was prompted by the National Water Initiative water policy reform, government investment in water saving and the need to deal with the problem of over-allocation.[21] The Water Accounting Conceptual Framework formed the foundation for the development of the Water Accounting Standards.[22]

The Water Accounting Standards were developed by taking into account the wide range of stakeholders that use water information. The Commonwealth government uses water accounts to measure progress on returning water to the Murray-Darling under the Murray-Darling Basin Plan. Water accounts are used to help market participants make informed choices about water use so that they can manage the risk of their transactions.[23] For example, irrigators may choose particular crops in line with forecasts for water availability that are based on water reports, or councils may purchase extra water from the market to secure municipal supplies.[24] Water account information could be used by government policy makers, lobby groups, regulators, consultants, academics and environmental organisations for decision making about a water project.[25] Water Accounting Standard 1 and 2 are voluntary standards that may be used in the public and private sector.[26] The true value of water accounting is that it allows information on water take and use to be benchmarked across all water users. These Water Accounting Standards also provided consistent definitions of water assets and liabilities.

The Comparative Analysis Table shows that water information in the Australian states is reported using the Water Accounting Standards. Water accounts based on the Water Accounting Standards may be collated by the Bureau of Meteorology, which is responsible for preparing annual water accounts. In comparison, whereas the Australian Water Accounting Standards are for all public and private water users, the New Zealand water accounting guidance has been prepared for regional councils only.[27] The guide includes examples of the various approaches taken by regional councils' collecting and reporting of water "accounting" data. This guide includes a reporting template which records consumptive and non-consumptive takes and categories of water for the environment.[28] The New Zealand water accounting guide would benefit from being expanded to all water users. There should be further research undertaken on whether the Australian Water Accounting Standards should be adopted in New Zealand.

Alternatives to the "first come, first served" method of water allocation in New Zealand

The comparison with Australia showed a significant difference between current water allocation in New Zealand and the extent of water law reform that has been undertaken in Australia. It is fair to state that New Zealand is lagging in addressing water allocation and finding alternative methods to allocate water to the environment, bulk water takes and other water takes.

In Australia, states can prioritise water allocation based on the different categories of water take. One of the difficulties in making comparisons with Australia is that each state has a unique approach to the naming and classification of water allocation. The difference in approaches is important to note in the comparative analysis because it means that the comparisons are not direct comparisons between Australian states and New Zealand. With regards to water allocation, the Comparative Analysis Table shows that states can divide up their water allocations by volume. The Comparative Analysis Table shows that bulk water entitlements for irrigation water or municipal water supply can then be given priority over other water takes if necessary. The distinction between water takes enables a prioritising of water takes according to water policy objectives. In comparison, regional councils in New Zealand currently allocate water under the "first come, first served" method, which does not allow for a comparison to be made between competing applications regardless of the size or volume of the take.[29]

The lack of strong guidance in freshwater allocation priorities is an issue for councils deciding water allocation applications. Regional councils are challenged by the fact that there is no distinction between the demand for water for New Zealand's national projects in irrigation, increased demand from municipal water suppliers and from other individual consents.[30] Councils are limited in their ability to assess the applications before them because of the "first come, first served" allocation method.[31] The current allocation method prevents councils from comparing one application against another or from considering other future potential uses for the same water. As a result, the "first come, first served" method effectively prevents water from being allocated to its highest-value use. Some councils are calling for "a robust set of criteria" to determine priorities for water allocation.[32] As has been shown, the current National Policy Statement – Freshwater Management 2014 (revised in 2017) still does not provide the "robust" guidance that the councils seek as it does not change the "first in, first served" method of allocation.[33]

There are a number of options that could help New Zealand implement more effective policy water allocation; however, these options vary in terms of their effectiveness. On the one hand, the National Policy Statement – Freshwater Management 2014 (revised in 2017) should be revised further to include more detail on regulatory tools to assist regional councils in preventing over-allocation.[34] This change would bring some minor improvements. On the other hand, there is a need for more extensive reform in the form of a specific statute focusing on water or natural resource allocation.[35] The latter option goes beyond amending the RMA yet again.

The Australian approach to address these water allocation problems has been to establish priorities by categorising water takes separately for "bulk water" takes (in the form of a distinct licence category or broader system of bulk water allocation), environmental water and other water takes. The other water takes are generally referred to as water shares or licences. These are simplified categories as there is no generic water allocation definition across Australian states. Each state has developed law to address these categories of water allocation as required under the NWI and Water Act 2007 (Cth). A core part of the reforms was to unbundle or separate water allocations from land. The unbundling process and how it led to the creation of different categories of water takes for environmental water, "bulk water" and other water shares and licences is examined in more detail below.

Unbundling water allocations

Quite simply, New Zealand has not unbundled its water entitlements from land. Consequently, there is limited scope to develop new water products or methods of water allocation. New Zealand needs to consider the value of unbundling with regard to the Australian experience in water allocation law reform.

Unbundling of water permits, i.e. separating the take and use of water from land, was an essential initial step in establishing Australian water markets.[36] Unbundling was included as an objective in the 1994 COAG Agreement and required that states unbundle their water entitlements.[37] Unbundling was required for two reasons: first, to facilitate trade in water markets and second, to improve the verification process of land and water information. Unbundling occurred at the individual state level. The Australian Productivity Commission has however been critical of the state implementation of unbundling at the individual state level, stating that "growth in water markets and the attainment of allocative efficiency have been obstructed by the failure to unbundle water entitlements on a uniform basis".[38] Nevertheless, the benefit of unbundling for Australia was to enable further policy options when allocating water[39] and the National Water Initiative 2004, which set the overall agenda for water allocation law reform and reinforced the commitment to unbundling.[40] The analysis of the Australian experience in unbundling shows the points that need to be considered before passing a law to unbundle water take and use.

Unbundling in Australia raised several concerns. There was a concern that unbundling and subsequent water trading could result in stranded assets. Water speculation was also an issue in terms of concern about the possibility that 10% of water could be sold to non-users.[41] The banking industry raised strong concerns regarding the potential effect of unbundling on financial transactions involving water shares. The banking industry questioned the lack of direction on how a water share was defined, the treatment of mortgages and how to ensure water access remained viable for irrigators so that they could continue their farming business.[42]

Before unbundling, the value of a farm for mortgage-lending purposes was based on the value of the land.[43] After the process of unbundling was complete, the value of land was clearly separated from the value of water allocated to the business owner. As a result of unbundling, the security interests in agricultural business loans also shifted. Banks were able to recognise the value of water allocation as a separate asset:[44]

> One consequence of unbundling was the creation of a water entitlement as an asset in its own right with a value independent of (and potentially greater than) the value of the land to which it was previously attached.

For situations where the value of water was greater than the land value, water provided the business owner with an additional asset, which illustrates that unbundling diversifies the asset base of agricultural businesses. The consequences for the banking industry are that unbundled water entitlements are more straightforward to mortgage and transfer.

The unbundling process in Australia also affected land valuations because the value of water allocations was separated from land. Consequently, the total revenue collected from regional rates based on land value declined. Councils had to develop policy to address the problem of lower land rate collection. For example, in Victoria, transitional provisions were included to ensure that the valuation of land remained the same for three years after unbundling. Councils in Victorian irrigation districts were provided with an $18 million assistance package to make up for the lost rating revenue.[45] New Zealand would also need to anticipate and address the potential changes to land rating and council revenue if unbundling went ahead.

Little attention has been paid to unbundling and its potential effect in New Zealand legal literature, although some account is taken of it in the environmental planning research.[46] Unbundling in New Zealand deserves further attention as it is an area for further law reform that requires action from central government. Unbundling would be the first step of comprehensive water law reform similar to Australia. It would allow the separation of water allocation into categories for bulk water, environmental water and other general water allocations in the form of shares, licences or entitlements. Ultimately, fully unbundled water allocation systems like that in Australia spread the risk of lower water availability across all water users. Hence the final allocation of water will vary on a seasonal basis.

General water allocation (water shares, licences and entitlements)

It can be seen that unbundled water allocation in Australia has enabled the development of greater options for water allocation. Examples of the different water allocation methods are detailed in the Comparative Analysis Table. For example, the states of Victoria, New South Wales and South Australia issue a water entitlement (generally referred to as a "water licence") as a permanent property right confirming the right to have water delivered to land. However, the actual water allocation is not equivalent to permanent water entitlement. The permanent water entitlement states the maximum volume of water that can be delivered to a particular site. The actual water allocation is a percentage of the total water available for that season and is shared between water licence or water shareholders. The exact methods and legal basis for calculating the share of the water allocation vary across states, which was evaluated in Chapter 6.

The Comparative Analysis Table shows that unbundling in Victoria resulted in three broad categories of water entitlements: for general water users (not a bulk water take or environmental water take); a water share which enables the holder to use the water; and water use rights for using water on defined areas of land and rights associated with the delivery of water for irrigators.[47] Victorian irrigators choose whether they wish to unbundle their water entitlements or not. There is a different approach in New South Wales where the water share is a part of the water licence and the water allocation is stated as a proportion of water available, as storage capacity or as a maximum number of units.

New Zealand irrigation schemes are self-regulated since the schemes were privatised under the Irrigation Schemes Act 1990. Once the irrigation scheme operator obtains a water permit, subsequent water allocation to irrigators is based on a contractual rather than a statutory basis.[48] The Australian experience in water law reform shows how regulation of water allocation in irrigation schemes can provide greater protection to irrigators. The Comparative Analysis Table shows that Victoria, New South Wales, South Australia and Western Australia all have regulation that determines how rights to water in an irrigation scheme are allocated. For example, in Victoria, the transfer of water shares involves a two-step process. First, the "Water Corporation" must approve the transfer. Secondly, the transferee must then lodge the transfer with the Water Registrar as part of the notification process under the Water Act 1989 (Vic). The first stage in the notification process requires identity verification.[49] The seller must also declare the value of water being sold when registering the water sale. If there is a mortgage against the water share, bank approval is required before the transfer can occur. New Zealand's unregulated irrigation schemes should also include these features. The Australian experience shows that unbundled water allocations are transferred with greater ease.

Bulk water allocation

New Zealand should consider separating bulk water applications as a separate category of water allocation. The Comparative Analysis Table shows the "bulk water" applications in Victoria and New South Wales are for major water takes generally involving dams for irrigation, municipal water takes or dams for water storage. For example, The Water Act 1989 (Vic) distinguishes between bulk entitlement holders and other water allocation permit holders.[50] One of these distinctions is that the bulk entitlement holders will hold water permits on behalf of others and the volume of water allocated is significantly higher than that for other water allocations. New Zealand does not have an equivalent recognition of "bulk water" or major water takes. Instead, all water permit applications received by the council are processed according to the "first come, first served" method of water allocation. Scant attention is paid to bulk water allocation for major water takes in New Zealand's environmental law literature. The need of other potential water applicants in New Zealand is a factor that councils currently cannot consider under the "first come, first served" rule, as discussed in Chapter 4. As a result, an application from a municipal water supply company is subject to the same priority rules as all other applications. As already noted, the priority rule for all applications currently rests on the time of application or the "first come, first served" rule.[51] This priority processing by time may put bulk water applicants at a disadvantage as the lack of certainty regarding water allocation may hinder further long-term planning.

The process for deciding whether the bulk water allocation is granted or not can be separated from other water allocation applications. For example, in Victoria, bulk water applications are lodged with the Minister for Water.[52] This statutory process shifts the decision making associated with the project away from the regional level. Consequently, the Minister assesses the bulk water application taking into account state rather than regional water policy and priorities. The Ministerial assessment of bulk water applications includes government policies relating to water allocation priorities and "the needs of other potential applicants".[53] In New Zealand, bulk water allocations could be suitable for high volume takes for irrigation, municipal water supply and electricity generation. The state policies for major water takes could then take into account other priorities that are important to consider in determining bulk water applications.

Environmental water allocation

New Zealand does not have an environmental water holder or an equivalent office with similar statutory functions to hold water rights for the environment like the Australian Environmental Water Holder. As has been detailed in the previous chapter, provision for the creation of the Australian Environmental Water Holder was stated in Objective 4(b) of the 1994

COAG Water Reform Framework. Under the Water Act 2007 (Cth), environmental water was recognised as a separate category of water and the Environmental Water Holder was established with special powers to purchase, dispose of or deal with environmental water in the water market.[54] Further environmental water was acquired through measures such as the Murray-Darling Basin Plan. The previous chapter showed that environmental water has also been acquired through buy-back schemes, trading and investment in water efficiency projects.[55] The recognition and aggregation of environmental water allowed the Environmental Water Holder to participate in the water market.

In comparison, New Zealand does not have a regulated water market. The Comparative Analysis Table shows that New Zealand does not have a number of the regulatory features that are a part of Australian water allocation law and policy. The Environmental Water Holder has been a part of the Australian water law reform experience over the last 20 years. The previous chapter stated that its establishment was driven by the implementation of water markets and a need to provide a legal status to environmental water. If further reforms to water allocation were to be undertaken, then it would be worthwhile to examine whether a role for an equivalent environmental water holder would be appropriate for New Zealand.

Summary

This chapter has provided a comparative analysis of water allocation law and policy in Australia and New Zealand. It critically evaluated the areas where New Zealand could learn from the Australian experience. The analysis showed that the Australian experience in water law and policy yields valuable lessons for New Zealand. New Zealand is in a unique situation where it does not have a dry climate like Australia's. Nevertheless, New Zealand does have issues not only with the full allocation of some catchments but also with the limitations of the "first come, first served" method of water allocation.

The most valuable lessons from the Australian water law reform journey relate to the foundational changes in New Zealand water law that are now long overdue. As a starting point, the recording and reporting of water allocation take and use require a more uniform approach. The Australian experience shows how a water register can be implemented and the range of information that it can provide in a transparent manner. In the Australian experience, the water register forms an important part of the water market information. Market participants rely upon the water register information for information about whether they should trade water. New Zealand does not have the same policy drivers for introducing water markets. However, it would be irresponsible to continue to allocate valuable water resources without full and transparent records of how much water is being allocated and to whom. Maintaining regional councils as the repositories for this legal water information is not viable in the future. Businesses relying upon water are using their water permits as assets. Financial institutions are lending money based on the information of the volume of water allocated. Thus, there is a strong argument for recognising the economic value of water by recording the information, with increased security for those dealing with the register. In this way, a water register would act much like the land register.

The analysis of the Australian situation shows that there are alternatives to the "first come, first served" method of water allocation. Australia has progressed further with unbundling from statutory water allocations, separating take and use to further unbundling so that new water products are developed and the risk of how much water can actually be delivered to a site (the water allocation) is spread across all water users. New Zealand has many choices to make about how to allocate water in a wider range of water products and how far it wants to unbundle water take and use. New Zealand should consider trialling further unbundling in irrigation schemes, which are currently privately administered and do not promote the transfer of water to other uses as freely as the Australian model does. Unbundling also strengthens the argument for a water register because there will be more information to record, information with layers of complexity that a range of stakeholders will rely upon. To implement more advanced unbundling will require promulgation of appropriate regulation by Parliament.

Another lesson that New Zealand can take from Australia is to pay attention to the cautionary points that have been emerging more recently. These relate to the failure to implement water law reform. There are concerns relating to water theft and a lack of transparent auditing of the implementation of reforms at the state level. New Zealand needs to be mindful of the underlying scientific debates relating to water allocation. These debates already exist in the form of appropriate scientific models on which to base water allocation decisions. The Australian experience shows that dealing with a lack of compliance, as evidenced with a lack of compliance with water metering requirements in Canterbury, cannot be ignored. Such problems need to be prominent in the mind of policy makers when reforming water allocation law and policy. A solution to this problem is to ensure that national water institutions with statutory oversight remain a permanent part of the water allocating framework. They should not be temporary institutions whose existence is subject to review. The literature on water scarcity proves that water allocation is a global problem. New Zealand is a country that has valuable freshwater resources. There is an inherent responsibility on the New Zealand government to ensure that water allocation in New

Zealand is not frittered away or "locked up" for uses when priorities may change in the future. The "first come, first served" method of water allocation is outdated and no longer suitable for a country experiencing economic water scarcity.

Notes

1 Cameron Holley and Darren Sinclair "Water Markets and Regulation: Implementation, Success and Limitations" in Cameron Holley and Darren Sinclair (eds) *Reforming Water Law and Governance. From Stagnation to Innovation in Australia* (Springer, Singapore, 2018) 141 at 142.
2 Cameron Holley and Darren Sinclair "Australia's Water Reform Journey – from Stagnation to Innovation" in Cameron Holley and Darren Sinclair (eds) *Reforming Water Law and Governance. From Stagnation to Innovation in Australia* (Springer, Singapore, 2018) at 5.
3 Cameron Holley and Darren Sinclair, above n 1 at 142.
4 For an account of the structure of water allocation planning in New Zealand see Chapter 2.
5 Resource Management Act 1991, Part 4 defines the "Functions, powers and duties of central and local government".
6 For a discussion and analysis of regional plans in New Zealand see Chapter 3.
7 Water and Soil Conservation Act 1967, section 14(4)(a).
8 *Keam v Minister of Works and Development* [1982] 1 NZLR 319 and *Stanley v South Canterbury Catchment Board* (1971) Planning Tribunal 463, 68.
9 Water and Soil Conservation Amendment Act 1988, section 3.
10 James Crawford "The Constitution and the Environment" (1991) 13 Sydney L. Rev. 11 and discussion in previous chapter.
11 See discussion on Australian Constitutional powers regarding water in Chapter 4 section 5–6.
12 Tranche payments were provided to those states that could show they had met key performance indicators in implementing the water law reform. See Council of Australian Governments The Council of Australian Government's Water Reform Framework 1994.
13 Productivity Commission Impact of Competition Policy Reforms on Rural and Regional Australia, Report No. 8 (Productivity Commission, Canberra, 1999) at 94.
14 The COAG Water Framework 1994 and National Water Initiative 2004 also stated that water rights should be unbundled to facilitate trading. See discussion in Chapter 6 "Australia" section 6 "1994 COAG Reforms – An era of Co-operative Federalism". In some instances, this approach has led to the development of further unbundling so that delivery shares are separate from the actual water allocation. Unbundled entitlements for the actual water delivered may be in the form of a permit or licence that can be varied. In other words, the licence holder will receive a percentage of the water stated on their water licence. For an example of this approach see Water Act 1989 (Vic).
15 See Matt Shand "Chinese company seeks consent to draw 580 million litres of pristine spring water" *Sunday Star Times* (13 August 2017); Chris Hutching "Chinese firm touts NZ's potential as a major bottled water exporter" *stuff.co.nz* (15 November 2018); Cate Broughton "Christchurch water protest attracts thousands" *www.stuff.co.nz* (9 March 2019).

16 Resource Management Act 1991, section 35.

17 The Supreme Court in *Marlborough District Council v Vining Reality Group* [2012] NZSC 11 confirmed a duty of care is imposed on Councils to provide correct information regarding water permits. In this case, there was a discrepancy between the actual amount of water under a water permit and the amount recorded in the sale and purchase agreement for a vineyard. Furthermore, if the Council is found to be negligent in providing information regarding a water permit, it may be held liable for its actions.

18 Eloise Gibson "When the river runs dry: The true cost of NZ water" *www.stuff. co.nz* (27 April 2017).

19 Parliament of Victoria Hansard (16 November 2005) above n 28 at 1947.

20 Jayne M Godfrey and Keryn Chalmers (eds) *Water Accounting International Approaches to Policy Decision-making* (Edward Elgar, Cheltenham, 2012) at 4.

21 Maryanne Slattery, Keryn Chalmers and Jayne M Godfrey "Beyond the Hydrographer's Legacy: Water Accounting in Australia" in Jayne M Godfrey and Keryn Chalmers (eds) *Water Accounting International Approaches to Policy Decision-making* (Edward Elgar, Cheltenham, 2012) at 22.

22 At Preamble.

23 At Preface [9].

24 At 22.

25 At Preface [16].

26 Australian Water Accounting *Standard 1 Preparation and Presentation of General Purpose Water Accounting Reports* (Commonwealth of Australia Bureau of Meteorology, Canberra, 2012).

27 New Zealand Government *A Guide to Freshwater Accounting under the National Policy Statement for Freshwater Management 2014* (Ministry for the Environment, Wellington, 2014).

28 Ministry for the Environment *A Guide to Freshwater Accounting under the National Policy Statement for Freshwater Management 2014* (Ministry for the Environment, Wellington, 2015) at 48. Refer to Table 5.1.

29 *Fleetwing Farms Ltd v Marlborough District Council* [1997] 3 NZLR 257.

30 *Tauranga City Council v Bay of Plenty Regional Council* Notice of Appeal on behalf of Tauranga City Council against Decision on Proposed Plan Change 9 (Region-Wide Water Quantity) (15 November 2018). The Tauranga City Council Submission to the Proposed Plan Change also stated that it is facing the lack of distinct rules for different types of takes, as Tauranga is a future urban growth area. The current method of water allocation does not allow for a comparison with other current applications or future demands.

31 Waikato Regional Council *Waikato Regional Freshwater Discussion: a Framework for Getting the Best Use Allocation through Time Issues and Opportunities* (Waikato Regional Council, Hamilton, 2016). The observations in this paragraph are drawn from this policy paper at 19.

32 At 19.

33 National Policy Statement Freshwater Management 2014 (Revised 2017).

34 Ministry for the Environment *A Guide to the National Policy Statement for Freshwater Management* (Ministry for the Environment, Wellington, 2014).

35 See Greg Severinsen and Raewyn Peart *Reform of the Resource Management System The Next Generation Synthesis Report* (Environmental Defence Society, Auckland, 2019) for proposed reform of the RMA including the potential to establish a separate Allocation Act.

36 Viki Waye and Christina Son "Regulating the Australian Water Market" (2010) 22 *J. Environ. Law* 431 at 437.
37 Australian Government Department of Environment and Energy *Intergovernmental Agreement on a National Water Initiative 2004.* (Australian Government Department of Environment and Energy, Canberra, 2004).
38 Australia Productivity Commission *Rural Water Use and the Environment: The Role of Market Mechanisms* (Australian Government, Productivity Commission, Canberra 2006).
39 Jennifer McKay (2008) "The Legal Frameworks of Australian Water: progression from Common Law Rights to Sustainable Shares" in Lin Crase (ed) *Water Policy in Australia. The Impact of Change and Uncertainty* (RFF Press, Washington, 2008) 44–60. New water products allowed the spread of risk across a catchment if there was a water shortage.
40 National Water Commission National Water Initiative. First Biennial Assessment of Progress in Implementation (Commonwealth of Australia, Canberra, 2007) at 3.
41 Parliament of Victoria, Council, Hansard (21 November 2005) "Water Resource Management Bill 2005 Second Reading" Speaker Stoney at 2252.
42 At 2252.
43 National Water Commission *Current Issues Influencing Australian Water Markets* (Australian Government, Canberra, 2013) at 16.
44 At 16.
45 ABC News "Councils back water rights unbundling aid" *ABC News* (27 September 2007).
46 Jim Sinner and Andrew Fenemor *Opportunities for separating the take and use of water in planning frameworks and resource consents. A Report for the Sustainable Water Program of Action* (Ecologic Foundation, Nelson, 2007).
47 The Water Resource Management Act 2005 (Vic) amended the Water Act 1989 (Vic) to introduce these changes. Parliament of Victoria Hansard (16 November 2005) "Water Resource Management Bill 2005 Second Reading" Lenders (Minister for Finance) at 1945.
48 Central Plains Water Limited, "Central Plains Water User Agreement 2015" Available at www.cpwl.co.nz/wp-content/uploads/Central-Plains-Water-Limited-Water-Use-Agreement-2015.pdf
49 Water Act 1989 (Vic), section 84J(2).
50 Water Act 1989 (Vic). Part 4 of the Act contains provisions relevant to the granting of bulk entitlements to water.
51 *Fleetwing Farms Ltd v Marlborough District Council* [1997] 3 NZLR 257 (CA).
52 Water Act 1989 (Vic), section 36.
53 Water Act 1989 (Vic), section 40(m).
54 Water Act 2007 (Cth) Part 6 details the establishment, functions and operation of the Commonwealth Environmental Water Holder. For a comparison of legal personhood of the Wanganui River and the Victorian Environmental Water Holder see Erin L. O'Donnell and Jullia Talbot-Jones "Creating legal rights for rivers: lessons from Australia, New Zealand and India" (2018) 23(1) Eology and Society 7. The Wanganui River legal personhood was granted as part of the settlement with a local Māori tribe. It does not acquire or hold water for the environment. In contrast, the role of the Commonwealth Water Holder is to acquire and hold environmental water allocations.

55 Commonwealth of Australia *Securing our Water Future* (Australian Government Department of the Environment, Water, Heritage and Arts, Canberra, 2010) at 6: Water for the Future has $3.1 billion for purchasing water entitlements to help restore the health of our vitally important rivers, wetlands and floodplains. In the Murray-Darling Basin, the Australian Government is buying back permanent water entitlements directly from irrigators in order to restore the balance between water for human use and for the environment. By the close of 2009, the Australian Government had secured the purchase of 766 gigalitres of water entitlements worth just over $1.2 billion.

6 Conclusion

The New Zealand situation

This research has shown that New Zealand water allocation is relatively unsophisticated in comparison to Australia. The allocation of water under the "first come, first served" method has led to problems with allocating water to higher-value use. Nor can regional councils legally take into account alternative uses for water. The lack of comparison with other applications means there is hardly any opportunity to prioritise one use over another. In some catchments, the demand for water has resulted in a goldrush effect as applicants rush to be next in line to apply for limited water resources. Fully allocated catchment are facing the problem of how to reallocate water. In this context, the Australian experience of water law reform can provide valuable lessons in how to implement water law reform to improve water allocation. The Australian water law reform experience is comprehensive, and it must be considered as a package of reforms.

The evaluation of New Zealand water allocation law focused on the policy gap at the national level from 1991 to 2011. It addressed the significance of the gap contributing to problems with water allocation. The analysis showed that, in theory, the Resource Management Act (RMA) and its hierarchy of planning instruments would provide a framework for resource allocation that allowed the resource users to determine how and when they would apply for resources, including water. Furthermore, it showed that adding to water allocation problems was the fact that during this policy gap, the development of water allocation plans and rules varied considerably amongst regions. This variation has contributed to the problems faced by New Zealand with over-allocation in some catchments, especially since some regions had weak plans for water allocation.

One of the key policy responses to water allocation and water quality issues was the establishment of the Land and Water Forum. The Forum identified areas that required further attention and made recommendations to address them. The Forum also stated that the "first come, first served" method of water allocation was problematic. The "first come, first served" method of water allocation is a default mechanism for determining water permit applications. The problem is that it provides little incentive for water transfers and can result in a gold-rush effect between applicants. The Forum clearly articulated the problems with water allocation in its Reports.

Some may question why the government has not closely followed the Forum recommendations concerning examining the potential of water markets. Part of the answer to this question is that the Forum was established outside the formal processes of developing national direction under the RMA. Hence the government was not legally obliged to follow its recommendations. That is despite its support for the Forum. From a policy perspective, the Forum Reports have influenced the national direction under the National Policy Statement for Freshwater Management, which was first promulgated in 2011. The analysis of policy development after the policy gap and of the National Policy Statement itself showed that measures to address over-allocation remained inadequate. The significance of this finding is that despite the identification of problems with water allocation, such as the lack of ability to easily transfer water to higher-value uses, further policy development and implementation remain slow. Specifically, there is a lack of national direction on unbundling, developing a water register, separate legal recognition of environmental water or re-establishing the hydrometric network.

The research recognised that New Zealand is at a crossroads when it comes to water allocation in terms of addressing water allocation law and policy problems. There appears to be a degree of inertia in addressing water allocation problems in New Zealand in particular. This may appear to be a contradictory statement in light of the policy work undertaken as part of the Land and Water Forum and the revisions to the National Policy Statement Freshwater Management that focus on water quality. This is particularly true when making a comparison with the lack of policy direction during the national policy gap from 1991 to 2011. However, when making a comparison with the comprehensive package of Australian water law reform implemented across states, there is evidence of inertia in New Zealand water law and policy development to make improvements to the current system of water allocation. New Zealand would need to implement changes to water allocation law and policy in one jurisdiction without the need to overcome constitutional barriers like Australia has grappled with.

The research questions posed in this book was focused on lessons from Australian water law reform. One of the limitations of the Australian water law reform experience is that it does not address the issues relating to water allocation and indigenous people. Further research needs to examine the implications of changes to water allocation law and policy in relation to the voice of Māori in water allocation.

Lessons from Australia

Australia has made an effort to deal comprehensively with its water allocation. The more recent reforms have resulted in a hard won commitment from states to allocate water more efficiently. The method of allocation generally involves categorising water takes based on their volume as bulk water takes, environmental water or general categories of water shares and licences. At the heart of the water allocation system in Australia is the understanding that the volume of water allocated is not necessarily the volume of water received. The water allocation system in Australia generally allows for the actual volume of take in water licences and shares to be adjusted by the state. The state reserves its discretion to adjust the allocation based on how much water is available in a season. For example, all water licence holders in a catchment may have their actual water allocation determined as a percentage of the total available water. At times of scarcity, this method of water allocation is able to spread the risk of a lack of water more evenly across water licence holders. The categories and rights associated with different types of water licences bring a level of complexity to water allocation that may not be embraced in New Zealand. The reallocation of water is then carried out through a market-based system. Through the market system, water can be purchased or sold as needed and the environment has equal legal standing.

The research on Australian water policy and law found that the constitutional structure of the Australian government hampered water reform in the Murray-Darling Catchment. It was not until 1994 that a comprehensive voluntary agreement between the Commonwealth of Australian States was reached with an agenda to improve water allocation through a range of policy tools including payments to states for implementing the reforms. The reforms are now facing a crisis of sorts with allegations of water theft undermining the extensive effort that has gone into reaching a consensus across states. The reform process itself may be on the brink of policy failure if states step back from their commitments to restore environmental water flows to the Basin. A further issue that has not been addressed in Australia is that of where indigenous involvement in water allocation can and should occur. Again, in New Zealand, addressing settlement claims in relation to water allocation should be addressed as a part of any proposed change.

It is important to recognise that Australian water law reform did not follow a linear path; however, there were points of significance in Australia's water reform experience. The first was the 1994 COAG Meeting where the Australian Commonwealth and states agreed on water allocation policy objectives. The second was the National Water Initiative 2004, which included agreeing to implementation of water markets and associated policy reform. Third was Commonwealth legislation driving change at the state level with the Water Act 2007 (Cth), which provided for statutory measures and timelines for implementing water markets, a water register, water accounting, water market rules, environmental water collation and the Murray-Darling Basin Plan to restore the health of the Murray-Darling Basin.

To begin with, one of the lessons for New Zealand is the importance of having one body to lead the implementation of reforms that is not connected to any other government department. The distance from other departments is necessary because of the transparent review function of the body. The comparison also showed the importance of national water leadership in Australia and New Zealand. In Australia, the National Water Commission was abolished to save costs. Yet its transparent review function and role in the implementation of the Australian water law reforms was praised by the Wentworth Group of Concerned Scientists. The recommendation contained in this research is that a body similar to the Australian National Water Commission should be established in New Zealand.

The importance of information has been apparent in the Australian reforms. Information about water take and use has been so crucial that Water Accounting Standards were developed as part of Australian reforms. While in New Zealand, there is a lack of appreciation for the relevance of water accounting information and how it can be communicated to a broader range of stakeholders. The experience of Australia in setting accounting standards shows that water accounting is central to developing water allocation policy as it also serves to bring common terminology and understanding of concepts related to water allocation.

The research identified what can be termed foundational problems with New Zealand water allocation. Any proposed changes to water allocation should be based on a robust system of recording water allocations in water permits. The research clearly showed that there is a lack of information regarding actual water takes and permitted water takes. The lesson from Australia is to ensure that comprehensive water law reform addresses water permit information. New Zealand's water permit information is regionalised and not centralised with a water register. There should be a consolidation of information relating to water permits in a water register. The significance of this finding is that it would provide improved legal recognition of the value of water permits.

This research has also emphasised that New Zealand must take heed of the comprehensive nature of Australian water law reform. The lesson is that markets alone were not the solution to Australia's water allocation woes. Markets were a means to an end and a part of a far more sophisticated approach to addressing water allocation than just implementing markets.

Markets addressed political and constitutional barriers in the Murray-Darling Basin to assist with the transfer of water across state boundaries in a more sustainable manner for the Basin itself by following the Basin Plan. Markets played an important role in the purchase of water for the environment. But to fully implement the return of environmental water, the environment was given legal recognition. The environment was given legal recognition with the office of the Environmental Water Holder. The use of markets to buy back water raised political ire in rural communities who felt unfairly burdened by the implementation of water reforms. The markets were implemented following the process of further unbundling of water allocations so that the rights to take, use and have water delivered could be traded independently of each other. While markets operate to reallocate water, water allocation itself does include the categorisation and prioritisation of water according to its use. The broad categories are bulk water (irrigation, municipal supply and storage), environmental water, and water shares and licences.

There is a lesson for New Zealand irrigators too. New Zealand privatised irrigation schemes under the Irrigation Schemes Act 1990 but stopped short of regulating irrigation schemes to provide irrigators with rights that would protect their access to water in irrigation schemes. Further regulation of irrigation schemes, like that in Australia, could also facilitate the transfer of water between different uses, not just existing uses. In the context of deregulation, the regulation of irrigation schemes may appear to be unnecessary interference in private matters. However, the Australian experience shows that regulated schemes can provide a range of benefits to those dealing with irrigation schemes. Underlying the regulation of irrigation schemes is the recognition that water allocations are a valuable economic asset for businesses. Irrigators are invariably operating businesses that rely on secure access to water. Providing irrigators with greater security with access to water and ease of transfer would assist in addressing at least some of the water allocation issues that New Zealand faces with the current "first come, first served" method of water allocation.

Furthermore, the Australian experience shows that valuing water allocations in the banking industry remains an area which requires further work. Yet, in New Zealand, there is a lack of discussion relating to the operation of irrigation schemes and the question of whether water transfers within them could be improved for irrigators. The Australian experience shows that further regulation of the schemes would ease some of the pressure relating to the lack of transfers of water allocation by providing greater transparency and security for irrigators than private arrangements may allow.

The comparative analysis extends the knowledge base regarding water allocation policy and law reform that Australia has undertaken and which

New Zealand has not. In some instances, the legal implications of the potential changes to New Zealand water law reform have not been examined in depth from a legal perspective. The potential areas for further action include further unbundling to assist with providing greater options for water transfers, distinguishing bulk water entitlements for municipal water, irrigation or hydropower and creating an Environmental Water Holder office. It is apparent that policy discussion alone will not bring change to water allocation. To make a change to water law, action is required to improve water allocation and put an end to the "first come, first served" method of allocation with comprehensive reform like Australia.

Index

absolute scarcity 1
ACCC (Australian Competition and
  Consumer Commission) 79–80
allocation: defined 5
*Altimarloch Joint Venture Ltd v
  Moorhouse* 22–23
Aoraki Water Trust v Meridian Energy
  32–34, 36–37
Auckland Council (New Zealand) 59
Australia: Basin Plan 142; bulk water
  takes 127–128; COAG (Council
  of Australian Governments) 140;
  COAG Water Reform Framework
  1994 72–74; Commonwealth
  Environmental Water Holder
  (CEWH) 79; Commonwealth
  government 122; dams 69; droughts
  71–72; environmental water 112;
  Environmental Water Holder
  131–132; 'external affairs power
  70–72; Federation Drought of 1895–
  1902 67–68; Murray-Darling Basin
  Authority 76; Murray-Darling Basin
  Plan 67–68, 126; National Water
  Commission 74–75, 111, 122–123,
  141; National Water Initiative 2004
  66; New South Wales water law
  and policy 91–94; property in water
  entitlements 80–82; regulations
  84; response to managing water
  4–5; South Australia, water law and
  policy 94–96; unbundling 111–112,
  128–129; Victoria, water allocation
  law 85–91; water accounting 82–84,
  112, 125–126; Water Accounting
  Conceptual Framework 83;

Water Act 2007 (Cth) 141; Water Act
  2007 66–67, 75–76; water allocation
  5, 140; water allocation law
  140–143; water buy-backs 78–79;
  water entitlement 129–130; water
  scarcity 2, 113; water takes 126–128;
  water trading (Australia) 85
Australian Competition and Consumer
  Commission (ACCC) 79
Australian Constitution: water and the
  drafting of 67–68
Australian Productivity Commission 128
Australian Water Accounting
  Standards 83

Barton, Barry 21, 33, 38
Barwon-Darling Plan (New South
  Wales, Australia) 94
Basin Plan (Australia) 142;
  Commonwealth Environmental
  Water Holder (CEWH) 79; return
  of water to the environment 76–78;
  sustainable diversion limits 79–80;
  see also Murray-Darling Basin Plan
bulk water allocation (New Zealand)
  112, 130–131
bulk water entitlements (Victoria,
  Australia) 86–87
bulk water takes (Australia) 127–128

Canterbury Regional Council 35
cap on water extraction (Australia)
  74–75
Cape Town: water scarcity 1
central government (New Zealand):
  water allocation 17–19

Central Plains Water Trust 34–35
Central Plains Water Trust v Ngai Tahu Properties 34–36
Clean Water document (New Zealand) 58
COAG (Council of Australian Governments) 66, 140; water information collection 125–126; Water Reform Framework 1994 72–74
Commonwealth Environmental Water Holder (CEWH) (Australia) 79
Commonwealth government (Australia) 122; 'external affairs' power 70–72
comparative analysis table 113–121
Connell, Daniel 75
cooperative federalism 72–74
Council of Australian Governments (COAG) *see* COAG

dairy farming intensification 27
dams (Australia) 69
Dart River Safaris v Kemp 34
Department of Sustainability and Environment (DSE) (Victoria, Australia) 88
domestic water takes 26
droughts (Australia) 71–72

economic water scarcity (New Zealand) 2, 113
EDO (Environmental Defenders Office of Victoria) 89
Electricity Corporation of New Zealand Ltd v Manawatu-Wanganui Regional Council 24
Environment Canterbury, water allocation 27–29
Environment Court (New Zealand) 18, 25; *Central Plains Water Trust v Ngai Tahu Properties* 34–35; *Fleetwing Farms v Marlborough District Council* 31–32
Environmental Defence Society (New Zealand) 59
Environmental Defenders Office of Victoria (EDO) 89
environmental flow limits 19
Environmental Protection Authority 18
environmental water (Australia) 83, 112; New South Wales 93–94;

Victoria 88–89; water markets and 90–91
environmental water (New Zealand) 131–132
Environmental Water Holder (Australia) 131–132; Victoria 88–90
'external affairs' power: Commonwealth utilisation of (Australia) 70–72

Falkenmark Water Stress Indicator 1
Federation Drought of 1895–1902 (Australia) 67–68
Fifth Report of the Land and Water Forum (New Zealand) 58–59
"first in, first served" 36; alternatives to 126–128; *Central Plains Water Trust v Ngai Tahu Properties* 35; First Report of the Land and Water Forum (New Zealand) 53–54; *Fleetwing Farms v Marlborough District Council* 31–32; New Zealand 111–112, 138–139; Taranaki Regional Council Freshwater Plan 29–31
First Report of the Land and Water Forum (New Zealand) 52–54
Fisher, Douglas 82
Fleetwing Farms v Marlborough District Council 5, 14, 31–32, 36
Forum, The *see* Land and Water Forum
Fourth Report of the Land and Water Forum (New Zealand): water markets 57
Fraser, Laura 38
freshwater allocation (New Zealand) 127; First Report of the Land and Water Forum 52–54; National Policy Statement for Freshwater Management 2014 54; National Policy Statement for Freshwater Management 2017 Amendments 58; Third Report of the Land and Water Forum 56–57
freshwater clean up (New Zealand), funding for, Land and Water Forum 54–56
Freshwater Management 2014 (New Zealand) 127

Freshwater Plan, Taranaki Regional
Council 29–31
funding for freshwater clean up and
irrigation (New Zealand), Land and
Water Forum 54–56

*Geotherm v Waikato Regional
Council* 35
global responses to: water scarcity 2–4
ground water 2

*Hampton v Canterbury Regional
Council* 36–38
Hauraki Gulf Marine Park Act 2002 59
Hawkes Bay Regional Council
(New Zealand) 56
High Level Plan on Water 3
historical hydrological information
(New Zealand) 16–17
Horizons Regional Council 26;
One Plan 27
Hydro-Electric Commission of
Tasmania 70–72
hydrological information
(New Zealand) 16–17; First Report
of the Land and Water Forum 52–53

IAF (Irrigation Acceleration Fund)
(New Zealand) 54, 57
ICM Agriculture Pty Ltd (ICM) 80–82
ICM Agriculture v The Commonwealth
80–82
Indigenous Australians 68
irrigation (Australia): New South Wales
91–92; regional plans 27–31
irrigation (New Zealand) 130, 142;
funding for Land and Water Forum
54–56
Irrigation Acceleration Fund (IAF)
(New Zealand) 8, 54, 57
Irrigation Act 1886 (Australia) 81
Irrigation Act 2009 (South Australia)
95–96
Irrigation Schemes Act 1990 (New
Zealand) 8, 142

lack of historical hydrological
information (New Zealand) 16–17;
First Report of the Land and Water
Forum 52–53

Lake Tekapo 33
Land and Water Forum (New Zealand)
16, 51–54, 138–139; Fifth Report
58–59; First Report of the Land and
Water Forum 52–54; Fourth Report
57; funding for freshwater clean up
and irrigation 54–56; Second Report
56–57
Land Information Memorandum (LIM)
(New Zealand) 22–23
land swaps (New Zealand) 56
lawsuits: *Altimarloch Joint Venture Ltd
v Moorhouse* 22–23; *Aoraki Water
Trust v Meridian Energy* 32–34,
36–37; *Central Plains Water Trust
v Ngai Tahu Properties* 34–36; *Dart
River Safaris v Kemp* 34; *Electricity
Corporation of New Zealand Ltd
v Manawatu-Wanganui Regional
Council* 24; *The Favourite Ltd v
Vavasour* 22; *Fleetwing Farms v
Marlborough District Council* 31–32,
36; *Geotherm v Waikato Regional
Council* 35; *Hampton v Canterbury
Regional Council* 36–38; *ICM
Agriculture v The Commonwealth*
80–82; *Li v Auckland Council* 59;
Mabo v Queensland 68; *Pierau v
Auckland Council* 59; *Southern Alps
Air Ltd v Queenstown Lakes District
Council* 34
Li v Auckland Council 59
LIM (Land Information Memorandum)
22–23
limits: Water Act 2007 (Cth) 76
Local Government Official Information
and Meetings Act 1987 23

Mabo v Queensland 68
major water takes: regional plans
27–31; Victoria (Australia) 86–87;
see also bulk water takes
managing water 4–5
Māori 6–7
Marlborough District Council 22–23;
"first in, first served" rule 31–32
Meridian Energy 32–33
Millennium Drought (Australia) 72
minimum flows 23–25; under RMA
25–26

Minister of Aquaculture (New Zealand) 18
Minister of Conservation (New Zealand) 18
Ministry for the Environment (New Zealand) 17–18, 123
Murray-Darling Basin (Australia): caps on water extraction 74–75
Murray-Darling Basin Authority (Australia) 76, 77, 94
Murray-Darling Basin Balanced Water Fund (Australia) 79
Murray-Darling Basin Plan (Australia) 67, 126, 142; over-allocation 69; Water Allocation Plans 96; water buy-backs 78–79; water policy 67–68; water-sharing agreements between states 68–69

National Competition Commission (New South Wales, Australia) 91
National Competition Policy (Australia) 73
National Development Act 1979 (New Zealand) 9
national direction 18
National Environmental Standard 15, 18
National Policy Statement for Freshwater Management 2014 (New Zealand) 54, 127; implementation 59
National Policy Statement for Freshwater Management 2017 Amendments (New Zealand) 58
National Policy Statement for Renewable Electricity Generation 2011 (New Zealand) 25
National Policy Statements 14, 18
National Resources Management Group (South Australia) 95
National Water and Soil Conservation Authority (New Zealand) 8–9, 24, 53, 122; minimum flows 23
National Water Commission (Australia) 74, 111, 122–123, 141
National Water Initiative 2004 (Australia) 66, 74–75, 125, 140
Natural Resource Management Plans (South Australia) 96

Natural Resources Act 2004 (South Australia) 94–95
Natural Resources Management (NRM) Boards (South Australia) 95
New South Wales, Australia 80–82; irrigation 130; water law and policy 91–94
New Zealand: bulk water allocation 130–131; bulk water applications 112; economic water scarcity 113; environmental water 131–132; "first in, first served" rule 111–112; freshwater allocation 127; irrigation 130, 142; Irrigation Schemes Act 1990 142; Ministry for the Environment 123; National Water and Soil Conservation Authority 122; Personal Property Securities Act 1999 124; response to managing water 4–5; RMA (Resource Management Act 1991) 4, 113, 138; unbundling 111–112, 128–129; water accounting 126; water allocation 5; water allocation limits 15–16; water markets 79; water permits 124–125, 141; water registers 123–125; water scarcity 2; water transfers 111
New Zealand Coastal Policy Statement 18
Ngai Tahu Properties 34–35
Ngati Tuwharetoa, Raukawa, and Te Arawa River Iwi Waikato River Act 2010 (New Zealand) 25
NRM (Natural Resources Management) Boards (South Australia) 95

O'Donnell, Erin 79, 88–89
OECD (Organisation for Economic Co-operation and Development) 16
Organisation for Economic Co-operation and Development (OECD) 16
Otago Regional Council Water Plan, minimum flows 25
over-allocation: Murray-Darling Basin Plan (Australia) 69

Palmer, Geoffrey 19
Personal Property Securities Act 1999 (New Zealand) 21, 124

Pierau v Auckland Council 59
planned allocation 19–20, 26
Planning Tribunal, minimum flows
24–25
policy gaps (New Zealand)14
policy programmes: Land and
Water Forum (New Zealand)
51–54; National Policy Statement
for Freshwater Management 2014
(New Zealand) 54; Water Act 2007
(Australia) 75–76
priorities for water allocation 31–39
privatising irrigation schemes
(New South Wales, Australia) 91–92
property: water permits 38–39
property in water entitlements
(Australia): *ICM Agriculture v The
Commonwealth* 80–82
Protection of Personal Properties and
Property Rights Act 1998 21

Queenstown Lakes District Council 34

Ramsar Convention (Australia) 70
Recommendation 57, Fourth Report
of the Land and Water Forum
(New Zealand) 57
The Reform of the Resource
Management System Synthesis
Report (New Zealand) 59
regional government: minimum flows
23–25; priorities for water allocation
31; water allocation 19–21; water
permits (RMA) 22–23
Regional Management Plan (Western
Australia) 97–98
regional plans: major water takes and
irrigation 27–31; water allocation
26–27
regulations (Australia) 84
Resource Management Act 1991
(New Zealand) *see* RMA (Resource
Management Act 1991)
Resource Management Regulations
2010 16–17
Rights in Water and Irrigation Act 1914
(Western Australia) 97
riparian system 81
River Murray Commission (RMC)
(Australia) 68–69

River Murray Waters Agreement
(RMWA) (Australia) 68–69
RMA (Resource Management Act
1991) (New Zealand) 4, 9, 113,
138; minimum flows 25–26; section
14 20; section 32 20; section 46A
18; section 122 21; section 136
21–22; transfer of water permits
21–23; water allocation 17–23; water
permits 33, 124
RMC (River Murray Commission)
(Australia) 68–69
RMWA (River Murray Waters
Agreement) (Australia) 68–69
Ruahine Forest Park (New Zealand) 56
Ruataniwha Dam project
(New Zealand) 56

Second Report of the Land and Water
Forum (New Zealand) 56–57
section 14, RMA (Resource
Management Act 1991)
(New Zealand) 20
section 32, RMA (Resource
Management Act 1991)
(New Zealand) 20
section 46A, RMA (Resource
Management Act 1991)
(New Zealand) 18
section 122, RMA (Resource
Management Act 1991)
(New Zealand) 21
section 136, RMA (Resource
Management Act 1991)
(New Zealand) 21–22
sector-based allocation: Waitaki 19–20
South Australia: irrigation 130; water
law and policy 94–96
*Southern Alps Air Ltd v Queenstown
Lakes District Council* 34
state-sponsored construction of dams,
Australia 69
statutory framework: New South
Wales, Australia 92; New Zealand
17; South Australia 94–95; Water Act
1989 (Vic) 85–86; Western Australia
96–97
Submission Summary Report
(New Zealand) 58
surface water 2

sustainability: response to managing
water 4–5
Sustainable Development Goals
(United Nations): water scarcity 2–3
sustainable diversion limits: Water Act
2007 (Cth) 76–80; water buy-backs
(Australia) 78–79
Sustainable Land Use Forum 16
SWOPA (Consultation on the
Sustainable Water Program of
Action) 15

Taranaki Regional Council, Freshwater
Plan 29–31
Tasmania Dam case 70–72
The Favourite Ltd v Vavasour 22
The Next Steps for Freshwater 58
Third Report of the Land and Water
Forum (New Zealand) 56–57
transfer of water permits (RMA) 21–23
Tukituki Catchment Proposal Board of
Inquiry (New Zealand) 56

unbundling 5–6; Australia 111–112,
128–129; New South Wales,
Australia 93; New Zealand 111–112,
128–129; South Australia 95–96;
Victoria, Australia 86, 124
United Nations: Sustainable
Development Goals 2–3

Victoria (Australia): bulk water
allocation 131; EDO (Environmental
Defenders Office of Victoria) 89;
irrigation 130; unbundling 124, 129;
Water Act 1989 130; water allocation
law 85–91; water entitlement 130

Waikato Regional Council, minimum
flows 25–26
Waikato-Tainui Raupatu Claims
(Waikato River) Settlement Act 2010
(New Zealand) 25
Waitaki Regional Water Allocation Plan
19–20
water accounting (New Zealand) 126
water accounting (Australia) 82–84,
112, 125–126
Water Accounting Conceptual
Framework (Australia) 83

Water Accounting Standards
(Australia) 125
Water Act 1912 (NSW) 81
Water Act 1989 (Vic) 85–91, 130, 131
Water Act 2007 (Australia) 66–67,
75–76, 141; water charges 79–80
water allocation 5, 129–130;
Australia 140; freshwater allocation
(New Zealand) 127; managing
4–5; minimum flows 23–25;
planned allocation 26; priorities for
31–39; regional plans 26–27; RMA
(Resource Management Act 1991)
(New Zealand) 17–23
Water Allocation Board (Waitaki)
19–20
water allocation law: New South Wales,
Australia 91–94; South Australia
94–96; Victoria, Australia 85–91;
Western Australia 96–98
water allocation limits (New Zealand)
15–16
water allocation policy gap 14
Water and Soil Conservation Act 1967
(New Zealand) 8
water buy-backs (Australia) 78–79
water charges (Australia) 79–80
water data: recording and reporting
125–126
water entitlement 5; Australia 129–130
water entity (Australia) 83
water extraction, caps on (Australia)
74–75
Water Holder (Victoria, Australia)
89–90
water information collection 125–126
water law and policy (Australia)
140–143
water licensing: New South Wales,
Australia 92–93; South Australia
95–96
Water Management Act 2000 (New
South Wales, Australia) 80–81, 92
water markets (Australia): National
Water Initiative 2004 74
water markets (New Zealand) 17, 79;
Fourth Report of the Land and Water
Forum 57
water markets (Victoria, Australia):
environmental water and 90–91

water modelling 28
water permits (RMA): New Zealand
124–125, 141; as property 38–39;
transfer of 21–23
water policy: lack of historical
hydrological information
16–17; water allocation limits
(New Zealand) 15–16; *see also*
water allocation law
Water Reform Framework 1994
(Australia) 72–74
water registers: New Zealand 21–22,
123–125; Victoria, Australia 87–88
Water Resource Management Bill 2018
(Western Australia) 97–98
water scarcity 1–2; Australia 113;
economic water scarcity (New
Zealand) 113; environmental water
(Australia) 88–89; global responses
to 2–4

water shares (Australia) 86
water speculation 128
water stress 1
water takes (Australia) 126–128
water trading (Australia) 85
water transfers (New Zealand) 111
water-energy-food nexus 3
water-sharing agreements between
states, Murray-Darling Basin Plan
(Australia) 68–69
Wentworth group: return of water to the
environment, Basin Plan (Australia)
76–78
Western Australia: irrigation 130; water
law and policy 96–98
Wheen, Nicola 6
World Heritage Convention
(Australia) 70
World Heritage Properties Conservation
Act 1983 (Australia) 71

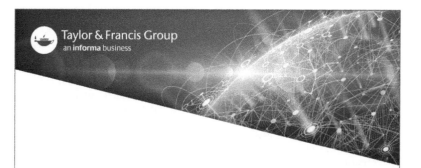

Lightning Source UK Ltd.
Milton Keynes UK
UKHW020811010822
406672UK00010B/1102